MW01617970

Coffee and a Smoke
Inside the wagon tent, 1980

Sorting Cattle

I never called myself a

COWBOY

A collection of short stories from the life and experiences of the author,

Jim Keith

Illustrations and photos by the author
unless stated otherwise.

Windy Ben Publishing

ISBN 978-1-7332111-0-9

Windy Ben Publishing
Tucumcari, New Mexico

Inquiries and feed back

windyben@snakebite.com

Dedicated to my wife,
Carole J. Keith

and to the many people
that encouraged me to record
some of my experiences

Thanks!

Forward

About a Lifelong Friend!

Have you ever met someone for the first time, and after a few minutes of "getting acquainted" talk, you just know there's a lot more to this person than meets the eye? You just feel there is a treasure trove of almost "swashbuckling, cowboy style" true stories this person could tell you. When you first meet Jim, you'll find him to be polite, reserved, attentive, and interested in what you want to talk about. But it'll probably take more than a couple of meetings to peel back the layers and find yourself talking to a seasoned cowboy, U.S. Army veteran, very accomplished artist – in more than a couple of mediums, an internationally known award-winning farrier, and much more.

A native of Maxwell, New Mexico, Jim grew up with a desire to cowboy, rodeo, and have a lot of fun doing just that. By the age of 17 he had hired on at a place where I was actually born and raised, the large and historic Bell Ranch; a ranch that dates back to the early 1800's, quietly nestled between Tucumcari, Roy, and Mosquero. Because of his desire to pay close attention, work hard and learn quick, a few of the more seasoned cowboys noticed his talent for horses, sort of took him under their wing, and shared tips, tricks and techniques for turning salty bronc colts into dependable, working ranch horses. Probably without even knowing it, in the dusty corrals working cattle and topping off these broncs, Jim had ultimately set the arc defining his storied career.

The captivating sketches and humorous stories Jim shares in his book *I Never Called Myself A Cowboy*, take the reader into the middle of the bronc corral, trying to wear a yellow slicker and many more "rolling in the floor" gut busting true events that he and others experienced in this fascinating way of life. They're the real thing; true accounts of events, lessons learned, and funny endings, involving real people, horses and places as lived in the saddle seat with a view of the world from between the horse's ears. These are the stories lived and written by my lifelong friend, Mr. Jim Keith.

Tommy Tatom

Preface

The stories in this book are based on the real life memories of the author. The chronological sequences have been altered in some cases to contribute to the flow, and clarity of the recollections. Sometimes the memories have gotten a little fuzzy and the details may not be exactly as it happened. Please consider these stories as entertainment, and not a precise history of my life.

After having numerous discussions with my peers of the time I have found that, often, their recall departs from mine. That is not totally unexpected as perspectives may vary from different points of view. If they have a more humorous or informative version I would encourage them to tell their own story.

Some of the characters names have been changed, and may be composites of several different people or horses, but every event is carefully related to depict what life was really like on the ranches and rural areas of New Mexico during the 1950's, and 60's.

The stories are written in the jargon of the times and the locations where they occurred. They may be difficult to follow for those that aren't familiar with the language usages of the time. For your convenience, there is a glossary in the back of the book. It may be worthwhile to skim over it before you start reading.

Table of Contents

Introduction

Shortly after Pearl Harbor was attacked by the Japanese, my mother gave birth to me, the last of her four sons. Our sister was born fourteen months later. Dad got called to serve in the Army, but soon got a medical discharge. He had lost an eye in a childhood accident, and supposedly couldn't shoot. During my military time, I shot "expert", but dad could out shoot me any day. Their loss was our gain.

My sis and I lived with our parents wherever they moved while following Dad's trapping and hunting job. The older brothers stayed with grandparents or other family members while attending school. They weren't around very much until my folks finally moved to town when I started school.

It wasn't very convenient for us to live near a school because the long commutes in those days were extremely difficult for Dad to do his work. Bad roads and unreliable automobiles limited the amount of travel. Dad often camped where he was working and we would join him when school was out. His camps were usually on private ranches where he was assisting with controlling predators of ranch livestock, and game animals.

He would take me with him while running trap lines for coyotes and bobcats, but some of the hunts for mountain lion or bear were a little too active for a tag-along kid. The times when I wasn't helping Dad was when I would go pester any ranch cowboy that would put up with me.

One of those ranch hands was a fellow known as "Rabbit". Never did know his real name, but that was of little importance to me at that time. In my tiny circle of acquaintances we could all go on first name or nick name basis. He asked me what I wanted to be when I grew up.

My rapid response was, "A cowboy!".

He said, "You're a pretty good kid, and may make a cowboy some day, but don't be calling yourself one until you understand what it means to be a cowboy."

He probably regretted that, because now I had a jillion questions. I would spend much time with him while he was doing evening chores. He fed the horses, and turned the dogies in with with the nurse cows. Then he would just stand and listen while they finished up their feed. The munching of the horses and the slobbering of the calves sucking were "happy" sounds to him. After that supper time symphony ended he would sometimes nail a horseshoe back on a pony that had prematurely lost one.

That may have planted a seed in this little kid, as much of my life since has been involved with shoeing horses.

He didn't give very many direct answers about what it meant to be a cowboy, but did say it was a state of mind, not the clothes you wore.

"I've seen old men in brogan shoes that could outdo any of those finely dressed fellows that rode the drugstore stools in town," he added.

A cowboy will know what a horse or cow is thinking before they do. He will be in the right place at the right time, and knows how to treat all animals and people with the respect they deserve as God's creatures. He honors the earth, its land, air, and water; and enjoys the beauty of sunsets and sunrises. He is in God's church every day while tending to the duties of a cowboy. On top of all that, he must make a "hand" by doing all he can when he can. Don't ride in front of another man nor holler at him. Hollering is what the drugstore cowboys do. These were some of the points he made to me. Tiring from my many questions, he told me that I couldn't get all my answers by asking; pay attention to what the good hands were doing, follow their examples, and try to figure out what the best response or action would be in any situation. I quit asking questions, but watched his every move like a hungry hawk – probably more disturbing to him than asking so many questions. It is a method I still use to learn something new.

Over the years I have struggled to understand what makes a cowboy. I've had the honor of being around some sure-enough good cowboys, and a lot of them that are heading in the right direction, ...and some that just try to play the part. It is still going to be a while before I get it all figured out.

In my life, I have ridden for some large ranches (and a few small ones), started hundreds of colts, managed a registered herd of Hereford cattle, played mid-wife to a thousand first calf heifers,roped plenty of livestock, shod or trimmed well over 100,000 horses, built saddles, bits, spurs, wore out many boots and hats, rode saddle broncs, and cutting horses, got drunk on many a Saturday night, but to this day if anyone were to ask if I'm a cowboy, I would say, “No, but I did work on a ranch.”

In reverence to the way of life that the cowboy typifies, I find it difficult to include myself, with so many shortcomings, in that exalted group. So, heeding that early mentor's advice, until I get it all sorted out in my mind, I will never call myself a “Cowboy”!

Tod Keith, age 17, Photo date 1930
My Father

Jim Keith, age 17, Photo date 1959
The Author

Photo by Robert Lougheed

Topping off Sacaton, the Bell managers horse.

First Day on the Bell

At the age of 17 armed with the exuberance of youth and a little on the job training I accepted a temporary day working job in Northeastern New Mexico on the famous Bell ranch.

I heard many stories about this old ranch that had been in existence since before this land belonged to the United States of America. One such recurring story was about how bad to buck the horses of the Bell remuda were and how many good cowboys were not "forked" enough to ride the broncs. The drifting cowboys who changed ranges, just to see what was over the next ridge spread these stories all over the American West.

As a kid growing up in New Mexico, we moved frequently as once an area had adequate relief from depredation we moved to another ranching area. We lived on many of these ranches and spent summers camped in a tent. So the outdoors way of life was all I knew.

The ranch hands and cowboys we met along the way were great at telling stories to young boys that would listen, some stretched the truth but, if they had a shred of plausibility I soaked them up like a sponge and the story tellers became my heroes.

The outdoors cowboy life was the life for me. School did little to introduce other cultures as most of my peers were of the same notion. In fact schooling reinforced the narrative of the cowboy stories by providing books on the subject. One favorite author was Will James, cowboy, artist, and author that was known for working on ranches from Canada to Mexico.

Will had spent some time around the Cimarron, NM, area near where I graduated from high school; however he was there a couple of decades before me. As far as I am concerned his books should be required reading for anyone with cowpunching aspirations.

As the stories go, he could ride horses so rank that Casey Tibbs (a famous rodeo bronc rider of the time) could not sit on the fence and watch Will without falling off the fence. I spent any free time in school redrawing the broncs and wild cattle from his books.

During those years of reading about and watching the cowboys doing their work and even helping a little at times, I felt ready to carry my weight and strut my stuff as a real cowboy. In reality as I look back on those years, I didn't know enough to even be aware of what I didn't know.

Yaqui Tatom was the wagon boss at the Bells. The pecking order on ranches at that time was the general manager at the top who usually attended to the business side of ranching. Next in line was the wagon boss who ran the day-to-day work and saw to the livestock operations although quite often their duties overlapped. On outfits that did not pull out a chuck wagon when they worked cattle, the second in command was usually called the foreman.

I was always partial to ranches that pulled a chuck wagon, but modern vehicles have all but made that obsolete. Nostalgia is the main reason for the practice to continue. Chuck wagon cook offs have returned to many fairs and rodeos but not many have survived in their natural habitat.

Yaqui was the epitome of the working ranch cowboy. Tall, lean, could sit a horse well, neat, polite, and could manage cattle, horses and men. He spoke very little....about fifty words a month was his limit. He was quick to smile and a smile from him was a better compliment than all the words in the English language. He led by example and never raised his voice. We did as he did until a word or a wave of the hand from him had us do something different.

His real name was Bill but Yaqui was the name that stuck; most think it was from the Yaqui Indians, but it was from yakky (incessant talking) which was in direct opposition to reality.

He was a favorite subject for the many photographers who visited the ranch. The well known Harvey Caplin exhibited photos of Bill in huge layouts in New York City and he may still have a picture on the Stetson hat box. Several artists also painted this cowboy.

The summer of 1959, I left a job wrangling dudes at the Philmont Scout Ranch near Cimarron, NM. I hit Yaqui up for a job, but the Bell wasn't hiring at the time. He would send word when they started taking on day workers for the Fall shipping.

A neighboring ranch was hiring so I took a job there, five dollars a day with bunkhouse and board. That was about the same pay as herding dudes but now it would be cows! Or so I thought.

We rode out the first morning to check on heifers that had been earlier moved to a new pasture. My mount was one of a recent purchase from Mexico with long heads and eyes that almost touched.

They were not too broncy, but really low on intelligence – a good burro would have been better.

The rest of the week was spent hauling cedar fence posts, unloading barbed wire, and shoeing the boss's horses. It appeared that there would be a lot of fence building happening soon, and he would be the only one on horseback.

Now I didn't have much money or even an automobile, but what money I did have was tied up in leather goods. Too much to even consider digging post holes all winter. So, it was with great pleasure when I saw a Bell cowboy headed down the road my way to inform me that Yaqui had a job for me, and he could give me a ride to the ranch.

I always felt a little badly about not giving proper notice but this was too great of an opportunity to miss. I got a good cussing when I quit, which I later learned that was pretty much what happened on this outfit when someone left. This was well rehearsed as the boss's wife stood in the doorway with a loaded six shooter. Apparently, unlike me, most of the boys seeking other employment wanted to batter his head a bit.

After this fellow became a widower we got along quite well and I even worked for him briefly again.

Early the first morning Yaqui roped a mount for me, led him out and said "Bell Cord" ......nothing else. The cowboy code said you took things as they came...so I did. This was without a doubt an improvement over the previous week's mount.

Without much ado I piled my kack on him, untracked him and noticed a little hump in his back when I turned him around.....but that was to be expected from a Bell horse. Pulled his head toward me and slipped aboard, eased him off a few steps and all seemed to be well.... But Bell Cord was a bit tight and he acted like he was walking on eggshells

Other stories said that the fastest way to get canned from the Bell was to spur or whip a horse so I proceeded to "talk" him out of doing anything that would draw attention to us. "Talking" was not so much verbal but often consisted of little tugs on a rein , boot nudges, or other distractions designed to change his mind from his desired goal of unloading his rider.

Yaqui soon kicked off into a lope as he led the crew north to gather the Big Flat pasture. Bell Cord could not contain his enthusiasm any longer, he downed his head and began to “crow hop” a halfhearted attempt at pitching that resembled a bird hopping or a ball bouncing along. Most horses will either soon tire of that and quit or go into an all out bucking, kicking fit. BC chose another option – he continued to crow hop for what seemed like miles. No amount of “talking” could convince him otherwise. Every time I'd pull him up and restart he resumed the crow hopping. I wanted to thump him but was remembering the stories I'd heard. We were getting behind but none of the others seemed to notice. It was up to me to keep up.

Yaqui pulled up to commence dropping off riders to start the gather; when he dropped me off he asked “Bell Cord a little fresh this morning?” He had already used up nine of his 50 words for that week.

As I rode along keeping track of the riders on either side of me that were about a half mile distant I came upon the La Cinta Creek in the early morning shadow of Huerfano Mesa. I aimed ol' BC to the sandy bottom where I would have an advantage in the contest between horse and man. As soon as the other riders were out of sight we got it on! As I kicked him off into a lope in the deep sand, the old pony downed his head and went bucking...a little harder now for the “talking” was over. BC had to grunt now with each jump out of the sand. A couple of flying “U”s with a doubled rope brought his ol' head up like a bobber out of a fish tank. A couple more runs through the sand just to test his memory and we were good to go.

I wondered why the horse breaker that named him Bell Cord came up with the “Cord” part of the name. Maybe it had something to do with a doubled rope.

We emerged from the sandy creek bottom and discovered that nary a soul could be seen. No one...just Bell mountain to the North and Huerfano behind me. I was lost.....didn't have the slightest idea where I needed to be. It occurred to me that could get you fired also. After a lot of head scratching I knew they didn't climb Huerfano mesa to the East so I headed BC west.

Not having any concept of the vastness of some of the pastures on the Bell, all BC and I could do was cover some country. I had visions of the cow crew seated in the cook house eating dinner while I wandered, lost, out on the lone prairie with a damned horse that made my plans go awry. We long trotted and loped (this time with Bell

Cord's head up and helping me search for another horseman). Soon a rider appeared in the distance, so far away I didn't even know for sure if he was on the same outfit.

With a big sigh of relief we made it to the roundup ground with the rest of the crew. If anyone was aware of my little lollygag no one mentioned it.

While I was hired as a temporary day worker for the Fall roundup Yaqui offered me a full time job and the horse breaking which paid a little extra. I worked there for a total of six years with an interruption for military service but started their colts for another three years after I returned.

Ol' Bell Cord stayed in my string for a year or so and never again got that "fresh" with me, but as younger horses came along I turned him back to the remuda for another seventeen year old kid to start on. Besides that Bell horses were supposed to buck...if they didn't then I considered them broke enough for the general manger to ride them.

That first day drove home the fact that you have to ride the horse you are given. And you need to be in the right place at the right time.

Making the best of every situation and self sufficiency is a great goal in life. I still hate to ask for help, even though I have to some times.

Cold Back on a Warm Day

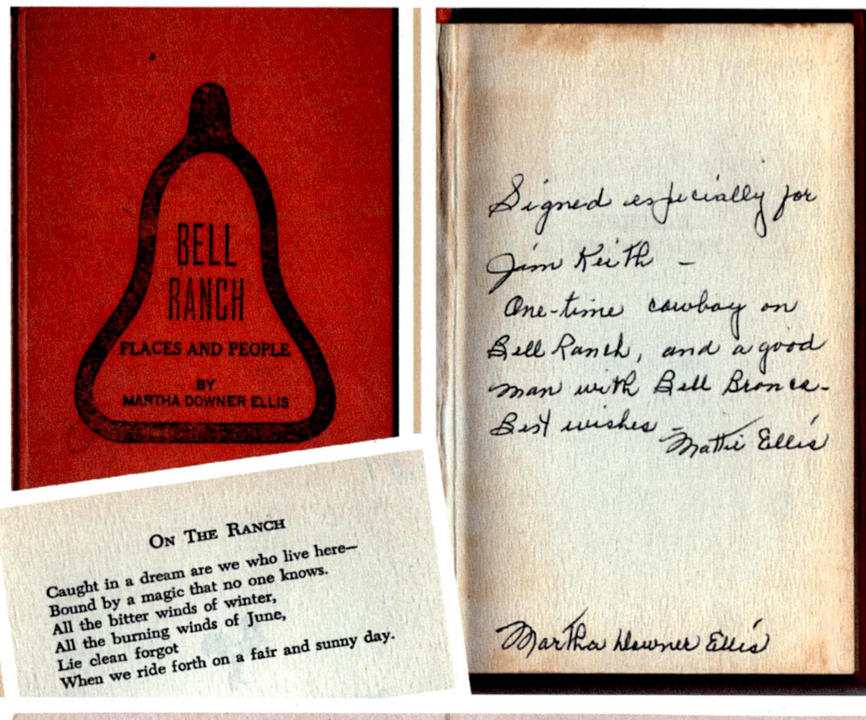

Painting by R.E. Lougheed -
Nov. 1960
Old Bell Ranch chuckwagon
team in foreground:
Duke & Custard, Tuck & Mustard.
Old cleanup team in center:
Bert & Chunky -
Bell Mtn in background.

Valued mementos from Martha Downer Ellis, author, photographer, and wife of Gen. Manager, George Ellis

Trip to the Doctor

Ralph and I saddled up and headed out bright and early one Summer morning to look for slick ears. In the Spring branding some cows with babies were missed during the round up. We would prowl the pastures looking for calves that weren't earmarked. At a distance earmarks were far easier to spot than brands or other evidence that they had already been processed so we didn't have to stir up the herds just to find the mavericks. This was always a fun thing to do, seeing the grass greening up and the general renewing of the land. Besides that, we often had to rope something!

When we located a slick ear we roped it in the pasture and branded it on the spot with a running iron heated on a little fire of mesquite limbs. While the iron was heating we vaccinated the calf for Black leg, ear marked it, and if it was a bull we made it a steer and dehorned it. We had to keep an eye out for the sharp horned old mama cow that was wanting to protect her baby.

Ralph had drifted up from the South where he had worked for several outfits, and after the works were finished he was hired on permanently. I'd been telling him about some Indian writing on some rocks near where we were. We made a little detour to see those large boulders on top of a little knoll. Among the petroglyphs was a sentence inscribed in Spanish which mentioned "pendejo". "*El que se ya pendejo Aqui en un*". My rough translation was "He who has been a fool is one here." Some times *pendejo* can mean stupid or coward. We thought that was a pretty deep statement but couldn't figure out why some philosophical conquistador or a more recent sheep herder had taken the time and effort to inscribe it into that hard rock. Anyway we proceeded to hunt for something to rope.

We split up to cover more ground and soon I got a glimpse in the distance of Ralph with his rope down and ol' Lightnin' (He got that name because he was a black horse with a crooked white stripe on his forehead) chasing a calf across a big tabosa grass flat. Those flats had a lot of well hidden holes in them. Well, ol' Lightnin' found one of them! They must have turned over at least three times. I hit a lope in their direction and saw Lightnin' get up and take a few tentative steps, but Ralph hadn't moved. I thought surely, he must be dead!

I rode up to where Ralph was sprawled out and I was greatly relieved to see him stirring a little. "You alright?" I asked.

He opened one eye an said "What the hell do you think? That horse just wallered all over me!".

He was grumpy, and grumpy was good considering all that had transpired. Then he started moaning and punctuating it with an occasional streak of profanity. Couldn't find any obvious broken bones or bleeding so I caught Lightnin', and asked if he thought he could ride to the house some fifteen miles away?

"Hell no!"

So then I offered to find him a big stick to fight off the coyotes while I rode for help.

It took a while to get him loaded on Lightnin' but he was now determined to ride to headquarters. We went most of the way at a walk because trotting brought on too much cussing.

About three hours later we made it home. The ranch manager gave me the keys to his big fancy Oldsmobile to take Ralph to the doctor in town some forty-five miles away.

Now, I had never driven anything but a four on the floor pickup and a tractor, so there were a lot of things I didn't know about on that car. Ralph was very relieved to finally get a little more comfortable, but it wasn't to last very long.

That car could run! As we approached a rim rock where the road took a sharp turn before dropping off the steep hill, my exploring all the little knobs and gadgets almost made me miss the curve. Those power brakes made us go around that corner sideways , first one side and then the other, and Ralph went into the dashboard.

As I was hastily apologizing I found something was under foot. Most ranches did not allow alcohol on the premises, but of course, the general manager was exempt from those rules. There on the floor boards was a full pint of good bourbon! Ralph took charge of the bottle and the rest of the trip to town went well.

At Doc Gordon's office, Ralph was a little wobbly going in but it wasn't from pain. He was even trying to whistle a tune! It was nice to see him happy!

The good Doctor was taking quite a bit of time back in the exam room, don't know if it had anything to do with the whiskey, but eventually Ralph and the nurse came out. She said, would we *please* go now. Ralph was walking better and I was confident we would soon catch that slick ear.

As was the custom at the time, when on ranch business, the last thing you did before leaving town was to check in at the Elk Drug Store for any last minute instructions or requests. Corny, the druggist, had stepped out for a moment but the foreman from a neighboring ranch was seated on a stool at the soda counter. He said the boss had called and the nurse had mistakenly released Ralph, and he should go to the hospital.

Back at the car when I informed Ralph of the new developments he reverted to his previous stance of "Hell no". Repeating the coyote threat wouldn't work here in town.

He crawled out of the car and started walking towards the ranch. Really wasn't too hard to catch him, and with the aid of a fellow on the street we got him back in the car. I gave the last sip out of the pint to the fellow for his assistance. Ralph kept referring to me as a "damned bull shipper". I think I lost a little credibility with him when I told him I could drive an Oldsmobile.

A hospital attendant met us on the driveway with a wheelchair and told me that they had received all the information over the phone and I just as well go back to the ranch. I wished Ralph well and asked who he wanted to have his saddle and bedroll in case he didn't make it. All I got from him as we parted was that one-eyed look I had seen earlier that day.

They kept Ralph in the hospital for three days. A week or so later we continued to snare a few more unbranded calves. The boss never mentioned the missing whiskey, and Ralph later told me the only thing he wanted to remember about that day was the new word he learned:

"Pendejo!"

The Anatomy of a Buck Off

or Pride Goes After the Fall

Many years ago when I was young and limber like the Ian Tyson song says, I used to like colts that pitched. That was in the days when many of the big cow outfits pulled out the chuck wagons for the Spring works.

A few weeks before they went out, the bronc stomper went to work. The colts were three and sometimes four years old. Their only experience with humans was when they were branded and castrated - not happy memories. They were pretty much wild, and harbored a lot of resentment for those memories, and their sudden loss of freedom to roam at will on the breaks and hills of their home ranges. They had to be big and strong enough to go with the wagon and carry a rider on the gathering circle. Two- year- old horses usually couldn't stand the pressure and pace of the round up.

My introduction into the cowboy way of breaking horses was by reading Will James' books, and a wagon boss, Bill Tatom, that was everything that I perceived Will James to be. Neither of these men spoke very much, were respectful of horses, cattle, and humans, and neither would be caught pulling leather on a bucking horse.

My swamper, Jack, was a young man of about retirement age who had spent a lifetime in the saddle on most of the large ranches of the Southwest, and, he was a story teller! His stories were a great window on the history of ranching and the men that rode the broncs and punched the cows before I came along. He did place a hand on the saddle horn when a horse could not contain his excitement and went to pitching with him, he didn't "pull" but rather pushed on the horn to take some of whip out of his weathered body. When the old pony picked his head up, they trotted off as if nothing had ever happened.

A swamper on a broke horse was the one who rode with the you while on a green horse to help get you out of a storm or, heaven forbid, to catch your horse if he suddenly jerked away from you while you were riding along admiring the scenery or your shadow. These three men (Will, Bill, and Jack) were about as important to me as my own dad.

One fine Spring day Bill and I loaded up a big wooden box filled with hemp rope halters with 20 foot leads and several one inch diameter foot ropes, some gunny sacks, hog lard, and some purple horse medicine and hauled it over to the bronc pens in the ranch's 56 Chevy pickup.

We didn't have horse trailers in those days so had to go back to headquarters and saddle some horses with a couple of other hands and rode back the seven miles to the bronc pens. The colts were gathered a few days earlier and put in a small trap of about 150 acres.

We penned them and commenced fore footing and haltering them. Bill was tied hard and fast with the long lead rope and when the gate was opened the bronc exploded out of the pen and was run or herded in the direction of the rocks used for staking them out.

Seventeen years old and I was totally immersed in the world of my heroes!

Next morning the colts were brought in one at a time, some of them actually would lead in after a night tied to a 200 pound rock and sometimes the rock was a long way from where it was yesterday! In nine years of this I never saw a horse seriously hurt, mostly some rope burns that were treated with the hog lard and purple stuff.

The lessons they learned were to give to pressure, and to not panic when their legs were entangled in the ropes. When the horse was pulling on the rope with its nose, it soon learned that the only way to get relief was to give in to the pressure. The rock was unforgiving and could wait all night for the animal to decide the right thing to do was to relax a bit. The rope was a foreign object to them but soon became a familiar part of their environment.

They were tied to the seven foot fence in the round corral and sacked out with some gunny sacks on the end of a lariat rope to allow you to stay out of range of the kicking and pawing. When they accepted the sacking, a hind foot was tied up and they were handled all over their bodies. A little tail trimming was done to remove any cockle burs and allowed the animal to relax a little after the mauling he just got.

Then the saddle was introduced and the weight of a rider was felt on his back along with a brief lesson in standing still while a rider mounted. I wasn't strong enough to "cheek" one but I could sure as hell make one tuck his chin while I got on. We used to practice mounting on broke horses with the cinches undone so the mount was done with a smooth gliding motion without pulling on the saddle.

The saddling was done with one hand while the other kept control of the horse's head. Most would settle down when they realized we weren't predators but when the restraints were removed and they felt the weight on their backs the old primal fear returned and they usually tried their best to buck you off!

The first saddling was the colt's time to do as he wished as long as he was doing something. Today's lesson was to allow a human to saddle him, mount him, and go! Never tightened a hackamore rein except for planned dismounts. The remainder of the seven days of "saddles" was when turning, stopping, and other requirements for a ranch horse to know were taught before entering the remuda of a working cow outfit.

All of this was done in about one hour a day because there were nine or ten more to ride that day. It was up to each cowboy to put the finishing touches on their new mounts.

In retrospect, this is similar to how the military conditions recruits to accept commands without hesitation; they remove your personal identity, your ability to choose, followed by a little shock and awe and you're ready to serve your country. Except bronc riders don't holler near as much as drill instructors.

Enamored with my success at riding broncy colts my confidence level exceeded all earthly bounds. Only one horse had sullied my record, a big chestnut colt that didn't waste energy fighting restraints and chose his rebellious moments well. He later found his calling in a rodeo string. By about the fourth saddle the treacherous rascal lulled me into a sense of complacency. He never humped up and did everything asked of him.

As I remounted after getting a cool drink of water at a windmill he blew! He bucked right into the wind mill tower, as I pondered the wisdom of riding it out or abandoning ship he made my mind up for me and took off for the wild country, without me. By the time Jack got him gathered up and brought back he had reverted to his sweet old deceitful self.

Jack observed "There's never a photographer or a pretty girl within fifty miles when a wreck like that happens!"- I was glad of that.

The ego recovered well and several of us went to town when the wagon pulled in. It was a little early to hit the bars so we decided to visit Calvin, the local horse trader. He was well known for running down every horse other people had, but if he traded for it, it suddenly became a much better horse than he had originally thought. Amazing how horses were made automatically much better and more pricey when he owned them.

Calvin had this neat little filly saddled and tied to a snubbing post in the middle of a large pen made from railroad cross ties stuck in the ground like pickets, it was a very good impact resistant fence. He said he was feeding her a lot of "post hay" in preparation for his first ride on her.

She was supposed to have been started under saddle and obviously not totally green as Calvin did not have any problems saddling her. Prior visits to this place usually resulted in me topping off a horse for him for free but this time he was offering me a ten dollar bill to ride this one.

Should have seen the red flag waving, but, heck, that was two days wages!

"Don't take your spurs to town, son. Leave your spurs at home, son," paraphrases Johnny Cash's popular song of the time. Consequently, unless there was a rodeo in town I didn't have my spurs or saddle with me. Calvin's saddle didn't fit me too well but, nevertheless, I turned the little mare around and slid on her back, she stepped off with a hump in her back.

When I asked her for a little more, I soon discovered she could change directions quicker than a patronizing politician. Then the little she-cat hit top speed heading straight to the cross tie fence at the far side of the pen.

I've had horses take runs like that several times and managed to come out ahead. The horse has several options: go through the wall, over it, or turn right or left. Stopping was also a choice but none of them ever did that, but some did run into it! As we were approaching the fence with her still gaining speed, suddenly her head disappeared! All I could see was the saddle horn, a few feet of dirt , and that massive fence looming in front of me. Her little suck back suckered me, I guessed a left turn - she went right.

What followed next was her lapping the pen like a rodeo queen saluting the crowd, my torso horizontal, my head almost brushing the fence, and, yes, it pains me to admit, my right hand was pulling on the horn.

After several laps it became apparent that Miss Priss had enough wind to continue this indefinitely and the centrifugal forces were too great for me pull myself upright. Many people have implied that I have a hard head, but I don't think it could have taken very many collisions with the fence posts to dispel that notion.

However, my main concern was that I was wearing my best Saturday night go-to-town shirt and I really did not want any used grass stains on it. Used grass is what is left over after it has been through the horse. I had to wear it for the rest of the weekend!

As with most problems that don't have an easy solution I tend to ignore them and usually they resolve themselves. That was the case this time. After what seemed like an hour of flying around on the end of a helicopter blade, Tinker Bell cut across a corner and the saddle started slipping.

I respect and appreciate Mother Earth but she was really giving my noggin a beating. When I got my eyes opened and focused I saw Satan's mare with the saddle hanging on her side calmly picking at bits of hay on the ground.

What started off as four of us there had now grown to over a dozen people; all were having a good laugh and some were making comments such as "You sure do like that nubbin", or "It looked like you were going to pull the horn plumb off that saddle". Within ten minutes every bartender in town had heard the news and were sharing it with all their clientele.

Later that night at the dance hall an old rancher's wife proceeded to inform me of my lack of personal hygiene.

"Clean up and change that filthy shirt. Don't you have any pride in yourself?"

"No Ma'am, I lost it all when I grabbed that saddle horn and still damn near got killed by that wicked bitc..., uh, beast of a horse!

"Whoa"

Apache
the Fair Weather Horse

The windmill man, Frank, when he wasn't busy repairing or checking a windmill, would hang out at the bronc pens every chance he got. He spotted a colt that I was starting under saddle and took a liking to him. This black coming-four-year-old looked like an athlete with a big rangy frame, and a small star on his forehead with a little "chrome" on two of his legs. His eyes were a bit wild looking and his flared nostril snorting could wake a teenage boy after a night of partying. He was an attention getter!

Frank, who didn't ride anymore, said he had a horse that reminded him of this one, and he sure did like him, "Best horse I ever had! Apache was his name!".

"Frank" I said, "this colt sure likes to pitch, and he doesn't like people at all!" He said that didn't bother him a bit, if I would just name him "Apache" he would become just like his old pet horse.

Since I hadn't named him yet and had considered "Geronimo" because he was well known as being a wild and cagey old Apache, I yielded to Frank's wish. This wasn't the first time Frank had pulled my leg; the name didn't change Apache's attitude one bit!

The horse breaker got the honor of naming all the colts he started, but the boss reserved the right to remove any and all profanity from the names if necessary. Once I had named a colt with a big bulging forehead, "Eisenhower," after our 34th president, but since he developed a hobby of running away with his eyes shut, I changed it to "Pecker Head". At the boss' suggestion it went back to the presidential moniker, which was promptly shortened to 'Ike" because he didn't deserve such an important name.

After seven saddles were put on them, the colts were turned into the remuda to be used during the Spring round up. The bronc rider got first pick and then they were chosen by seniority of the crew. Now, seven hours of riding didn't make a finished horse, that was up to whoever got the horse in his string. I was just supposed to get most of the buck out of them and teach them to stand while saddled and allow one to aim him in the general direction you wanted to go.

Apache was my first pick because he still had quite a bit of buck left in him. He wasn't too hard to saddle but required frequent re-aiming. After about six months Apache and I were getting along pretty well, and, sometimes we could go a whole day without putting on a rodeo show. He was a joy to ride when you had country to cover and could catch a cow quickly (he had to get pretty close to one for me to rope it). His energy level would still be high at the end of day which was definitely better than having to pedal a tired or lazy horse all day. In fact, he often felt energetic enough to to test my energy at quitting time. He never bucked me off, but I sure didn't get much sleep while riding him.

At that time the wagon boss let me have sixteen horses in my string. Most were known to buck people off, if I could improve their manners they wouldn't go to the horse sale. My pets weren't ridden very much or not at all, but still took a week or so to get around to all of them, even if you were riding two a day. Often during the works we caught horses three times a day. Those horses stayed pretty frisky with a week's rest.

Part of my rig was a waist length yellow slicker that was almost always dead weight to pack around; wore out several tied to the back of the cantle, but never when using it for its intended purpose. This old Southwest ranch country didn't see very much rainy weather.

Until now it had never seriously rained while old Apache and I were enjoying our time together. What few little clouds that sprinkled near us were small enough to ride around. But this cloud rapidly approaching looked like a gully washer with some hail in it!

Thought I had better get slickered up, but didn't dare try to put it on while mounted, so I got down and untied it and when Apache realized what he had been carrying on his back he made a serious attempt to jerk away from me. Then he wouldn't let me approach him wearing that slicker.

It was raining now, but I pulled the slicker off and managed to get him hobbled. All the horses on that outfit were hobble broke, we never tied a horse by the reins. I donned the slicker again and planned on mounting him and then use the piggin' string that had been tied to the slip knot on the rope hobbles to release his front feet and we would be on our merry way.

As I neared him he reared and struck at me with both front feet almost getting the hobbles over my neck. Every time I got close to him he would strike out at me, narrowly missing my head. Really didn't want to be in that predicament, as he could have gotten me down and dragged me around in the fresh mud. It was raining harder now. The slicker was leaking a little, but it didn't matter as I was already wet so I just hunkered down to plan my next move.

Eventually the rain let up and I was wondering if it would be best just to leave the slicker and pick it up later, but my partner rode up and he snubbed Apache up to his saddle horn and we managed to get the slicker tied back on the saddle.

We finished our little prowl, the sun came out, and I was almost dry by the time we got back to the home corral. I was determined to get that little score settled with Apache because it is not very comfortable to ride for hours with soggy underwear.

The home corral was about 80 feet square and made from rough sawn 2 X 12 lumber and built to last. With my slicker draped over the top of the fence. Apache and I took several running laps around the pen and when I got the chance, I grabbed that slicker off the fence and whopped ol' Apache over the head with it, something I had done quite a few times on other colts using a denim jacket. It was kind of like sacking them out while you were riding them. Sacking is a good way to habituate a nervous colt to a non-painful stimulus. They usually settle down and accept it when they realize it is not going to hurt.

Apache's hatred of yellow, or me dressed in yellow, had been grossly under estimated. He was squealing and pitching. About five good high jumps and he collided with the big heavy gate. I could hear the timber cracking and breaking. Splinters were flying, but we didn't burst through to the outside. Instead, Apache bounced back and went over backwards. I had squirmed over to one side of him and the slicker was on the other side. Quickly regaining his feet and still squealing, Apache lit into that slicker, pawing and biting until it was destroyed. Sure was thankful I wasn't wearing it! I got out of his way and let him work out his frustrations!

Apache stayed in my string for another year until I left the ranch. I went rodeoing and Apache went to the horse sale. Never heard what happened to him. Frank was terribly disappointed that I couldn't ever get him as gentle as his Apache was. Gentle just didn't fit him.

The whole year after that incident every time I caught Apache, my saddle did not have my brand new slicker tied on it and I carefully checked the sky for any sign of rain.

If it was cloudy, Apache got the day off!

Idle Hands and Minds

While the wagon was out, especially in the spring there was some time for relaxing, story telling, or just plain orneriness. The cow work was done early in the day to avoid the heat in the afternoon. Branding was pretty stressful on the calves, so no need to contribute more to their troubles by wallering them around during the hundred degree temperature. This high desert life zone was like most desert areas that had cool nights and hot afternoons.

Man and beast shaded up during the "siesta" time, but napping was a risky activity. Nothing was more tempting than a soundly sleeping puncher. A prime target for some of the rowdies in the crew to engage in some mischief just to kill the time or break the monotony. While many accounts of the things that were perpetuated upon the hapless fellow that drifted off to sleep on these afternoons are not fit for print, I will mention this. A favorite was to hobble him or tie a foot to a tent stake and holler "Snake" or "Fire". Often there may be a small fire to enhance the experience. My sympathies to the fellow that went to sleep with his mouth wide open and awoke to find a sour dill pickle stuck in his mouth; no telling what was going through his groggy mind. Besides even if you were asleep and not in your bedroll, you were still subject to the wagon rules.

There was "Wagon Etiquette" enforced by the cook. His job was to keep the crew fed, and healthy. It was a challenge to keep the cleanliness of the cooking area up to par without refrigeration, and sometimes not much wash water. Horses were seldom welcomed in the near vicinity of the food preparation area; they were hobbled about fifty yards away. Except for the wagon boss, the cook had total control over the activities that happened within the area of the wagon. A serious breach of the established rules could result in a "chapping" if so dictated by the cook who was also judge and jury.

Different cooks had a variety of rules, and some were kinder than others, but most were grouchy. Their work day was the longest of all. They had to wake the hoodlum and the horse wrangler, then get breakfast going. All this was done well before the sun came up, and, of course he and his helper, the hoodlum, were the last to bed after the evening meal. It was a good idea to not irritate the cook.

The most serious rules concerned sanitation. Flatulence was not allowed within the tent or fly stakes. I doubt that it ruined the meat but it sure could ruin the atmosphere. Remember, beans were a common menu item. There was an exception; once one had crawled into his bedroll it was usually overlooked, hence the term for a bedroll was often “fartsack”.

Women were not common at the wagon except sometimes on Sunday, they might have lunch with the crew. It was pleasure to have them there as most of the horseplay was held in check, everybody was on their best behavior. Besides, their desserts were usually much better than what the wagon cook made. At times a lady photographer may show up while the work was going on, but they usually didn't make it for breakfast to give the boys time for their morning rituals. If you will notice you will not see very many early morning shots of chuck wagon life.

If a fellow had to “water the daisies” it was fifty paces from the tent stakes. If he “went to see a man about a horse” it was a hundred steps. Someone walking smartly away from the wagon and counting their steps was an invitation to mind your own business, but if there was some doubt about the correctness, the cook could call a recount. The longest legged puncher was the one to do the recount. Some could achieve a six foot stride. In fact, one fellow had such long legs most of us would catch a horse and ride over the hill to take care of business. Remember what I said about irritating the cook.

Once when the wagon was camped at the Mule pasture between Medio and Huerfano Mesa on the Bell ranch, one of the boys made an interesting find. There was a small diversion dam to spread the rain run off over a larger area of grass land. It was about one hundred and fifty yards from the wagon – a perfect place for a horse trade, and afforded a bit of privacy too!

A day worker had squatted in the shade of a large mesquite bush, and in lieu of a magazine to read, he began to study the ground around him. There in front him was a couple of old coins. He finished his business and scratched around a little more. His search turned up a few more coins. Proud of this discovery, he returned to the shade of the wagon fly, to show off the loot.

Curiosity got most of the crew to the spot and to digging around, careful to avoid the zone of repugnance around the deposit left by the finder. All told, we found $2.85 in coins, and if memory serves me right, the newest one was dated 1885. We gave all the coins to the finder that claimed to be a collector. He researched the value, and later claimed they were insignificant in value (it was reported that he got a brand new car soon after). Probably just a coincidence because he was making good money day working – five dollars a day.

I profited from the treasure hunt with the finding of a small gold wedding band. Our conjecture of the events from this situation was that some old time cowpuncher from the days of open range had lost his coin purse. While the money may have represented several days work, it could be replaced, but the ring may have been a much bigger loss. Anyway, I hope the man that lost it so many years ago is happy with my stewardship of the ring. I kept it for several years, but when my Grandma lost her wedding band, I let her have it. She didn't want to make her debut in heaven without a ring on her finger. She was buried with the ring, and, I hope my Grandpa and the person that originally owned it are pleased with our decision.

It is said that some cooks would tie a white towel to the tent ropes to give the boys a heads up that there were women in camp, but I never did see that. If there was an extra vehicle at the wagon we pretty much suspected there may be a female visitor and took the necessary precautions. That rule may have come about later when there would be quite a few pickups or cars parked around the camp. In the old days, most of time there was a white towel hanging near the wash pan, but after ten or eleven hands rinsed off, the towel usually took on a brownish gray tint. A bright white towel would have been a good attention getter!

Had a new rule imposed on me by a modestly qualified cook: Never, ever, grease your leggings with a piece of his roast beef! I thought I was doing him a favor so he wouldn't have to dig a hole to bury it for the coyotes to dig up later.

Some of those hot afternoons were used for "pawing your nest" or airing out the old fartsack. Most of a fellow's personal items were kept in the bedroll, (no suitcases allowed) and needed to be rearranged or certain items located so they could be found in the dark. You didn't have much time to get your coffee and biscuit down and go call for your horse.

One such nest cleaning afternoon we got a surprise. A young gullible fellow had been warning the crew about putting a snake in his bed and had promised dire consequences if we did. The gauntlet had been dropped, but a snake wasn't readily available. Eventually the hoodlum killed a big bull snake shaded up underneath the wagon. Cookie was deathly afraid of reptiles.

We got the snake bedded down in this guy's bed while he was off seeing a man about a horse. Everybody that knew about this little shenanigan went to bed early and lay awake listening for the explosion. The victim got in bed, restlessly squirming around and taking a lot of time to get settled. We waited patiently, but nothing was happening. Then he began to snore! We thought he must have gotten wind of our scheme and removed the corpse, the joke was on us now.

A week or so later he was rummaging in the bed and found the ripest dead snake I'd ever seen. He was naturally a bit upset but we got him convinced that the snake must have crawled into his bed and gotten smothered. I think he needs an award for the longest period of sleeping with an actual snake. Of course, he got a lot of ribbing about his bed being too toxic for even a snake to live in there.

While we are on the subject of snakes, our cookie who was afraid of snakes told us once that he was asleep in is bed roll and woke up to find a large coon tail rattler coiled up on his chest. He dropped the subject right there and started to walk away. Knowing that there had to be more to the story, one fellow asked "What did you do? There wasn't anything sticking out of bed other than your head. How did you knock him off?"

"Why, I just went back to sleep and when I woke up later, he was gone." Even the gullible guy knew that was bragging!

Another hot afternoon, two hands rode back into camp after they had finished a little prowl to keep the already processed cattle from mixing with the bunch we were going to gather in the morning. They announced that they had just killed the biggest rattlesnake in the history of this country, and it was just over the hill from the wagon camp. They kind of implied that there may be more big snakes there.

"Must of been seven feet long." one of them said.

A couple of us headed for our hobbled horses. When they asked where we were going, I replied , "We gotta go see that snake!"

"Well, you better hurry, when we left, this hot sun was shrinking that ol' snake pretty fast!"

One more snake story before we move on. On another ranch there were two hands, a father and his son, who were great snake handlers. They would stomp a big rattler or step on his head, pick it up by the tail and pop his head off just like popping a whip. I always wanted to do that, but my knees got wobbly when I got too close to one.

I was riding drag one day and we drove a pretty good sized bunch of cattle over a young snake about sixteen inches long. It was pretty upset about all those cows walking on him, and was on the fight. Its four or five rattles were just a blur as it continued to display its displeasure. This was my chance to enhance my reputation by stomping a mean snake. The rascal feinted to the right then ducked to the left. My Blucher boot missed the lucky snake, and it hung a fang in the inside edge of my leggings. Kicking didn't seem to work at dislodging the viper, so the next thing was to pull an all out bucking, kicking, runaway. I don't know what happened to the snake, but I swear I could feel him crawling around in my pants for the rest of the day. I'm a competitive person but I don't compete in anything that involves snakes now. Which brings us to our next subject.

Toilet paper was a scarce commodity at some wagons. The rest of the world was using old Monkey Ward or Sears & Roebuck catalogs in out houses on the ranches and farms, but, at the wagon those modern niceties were not to be had. If you have been there or are a modern day survivalist you already know this, but others may find these suggestions helpful.:

Grass was often available. Green was better than dry – a little gentler and less stickery.

Sun flower leaves covered a lot area but left a sticky residue.

Cocklebur leaves, not often available but worked well. The big leaves had plenty of "tooth" to remove the most stubborn stain.

Sticks and twigs were not really effective, usually used to smear it around to make it dry faster.

Mesquite leaves were similar to grass.

Rocks were about like sticks but even less absorbent.

Dry corn cobs were great but not commonly found around wagon camps.

Turpentine weed was to be avoided. It is a very common plant on many Southwest ranches and very easy to harvest a handful or two, but remember, it was called "turpentine" for a reason. Also, the tiny little stickers were almost impossible to remove from your body or clothing. The gullible person mentioned earlier can attest to the veracity of this statement.

It may be time to change the topic here.

One fine Spring day we were camped at the Upper Seco and had several hours of remaining daylight. So Butch and I decided to ride up to the head of Medio Canyon and do a little exploring. Butch had been raised on a neighboring ranch and was helping us with the branding. His dad had once been the horse boss of this ranch back in the 1940's before it had been split up and sold into several parcels. When the split came Butch's dad became the manager of one of the parcels.

Butch related the story told to him by his dad about the horse wrangler that was with us now. Old Harry had worked for this outfit many times and gotten fired the same number of times but if we were short handed we could always count on him to come wrangle the horses for us.

Harry didn't talk much, when he responded to any one's attempt at conversation it was with grunts. He kept to himself and was constantly reading a paper back book. He didn't ever bother anybody and never caused any trouble except maybe when he would go to sleep while reading and let his horses stray, and we would have to help him round them up. He was an enigma to us, even though he had been in the area for over twenty years, he still had a New Jersey accent and no one knew anything about his past.

The story went, that back when he first worked there his duties were as a line rider or fence rider to keep watch over and repair the ranch's boundary fences. He would ride from the ranch headquarters in the early morning and return at supper time. He would take some books and a can of beans or tomatoes for lunch. It may have been the books that aroused the big boss's suspicions. The boss had an airplane to check out the ranch. One day he spotted Harry's horse hobbled on a small bench of land at the head of Medio Canyon and Harry napping in a little cave. Harry had to roll his bed and catch a ride to town that evening.

Finding Harry's cave some fifteen years later was Butch's and my objective that afternoon. The description was pretty accurate and it wasn't very long until we were looking back into history. The cave was about eight feet deep by ten feet long with a nice sandy bottom from the decomposition of the sandstone rock. We removed some sand and found what appeared to be some bear grass (Yucca) plants that had been laid out to make a nice little pallet. Several rusty tin cans may have been the lunch containers. It sure looked like a good place to spend a day reading and napping!

On the way back to the wagon we were trying to figure out how to get Harry to open up with us. We might learn a little more about this mysterious fellow. Butch found some change in his pocket that was minted in the mid forties. We thought we had found our hook.

Harry had already turned the horses into the trap (small pasture) for the night. The night horse was saddled and standing hobbled in the rope corral where he would be ready to go in the wee hours of the morning. We took care of our horses and headed for the wagon where cookie was starting to lay out supper.

Harry was taking advantage of the last remaining light to read. We sat down next to him and began discussing our evening for his benefit even though he didn't appear to be listening. Finally we just asked him outright if he knew anything about that cave. Never taking his eyes off the book he grunted incoherently. Butch pulled the change out of his pocket and we began to talk about all the money we found in that cave.

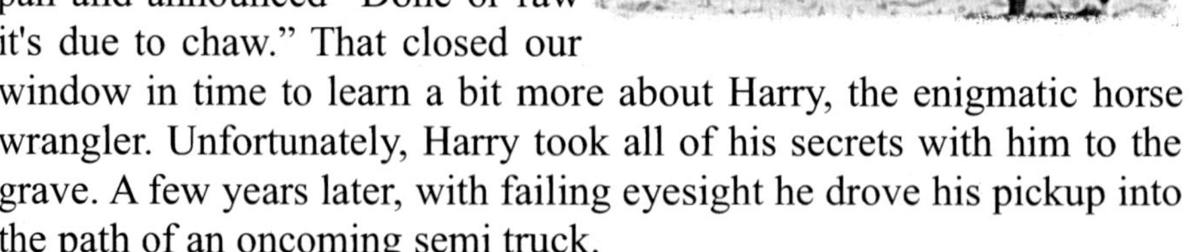

The book came down, and he looked at Butch, "Lemme see" and grabbed the coins out of Butch's hands. Harry scrutinized the money for about a minute then snorted "Huh!", returned it and went back to reading. I guess he couldn't identify the coins as his. The cook went to banging on a pan and announced "Done or raw it's due to chaw." That closed our window in time to learn a bit more about Harry, the enigmatic horse wrangler. Unfortunately, Harry took all of his secrets with him to the grave. A few years later, with failing eyesight he drove his pickup into the path of an oncoming semi truck.

Branding was hot, dirty work. Unless you were dragging calves to the fire you were right in the middle of the smoke, blood, manure, and dirt. After a few days of that most of the boys were about as ripe as gullible guy's snake. The stock tanks afforded some relief, but what really hit the spot was taking a long satisfying dip in the huge reservoir that joined the ranch. We would swim our horses for a while , then hobble them on some choice lakeside grass and go skinny dipping, or I should say skivvy dipping – we were a modest bunch. Most of us could swim but there is always one desert dweller that had never been in water up to his waist.

The lake was basically a dammed up canyon with many little side canyons running into it. One of those little canyons was about a hundred and twenty yards of deep water with another fifty yards of wading water. The nice little sandy beach on the other side sure looked inviting, especially since this side was a mud flat. The swimming challenged fellow wanted to go as well so we found a good sized driftwood log for him to kick his way across. We got across and made many tracks in the sand before we realized we better be heading back to the wagon.

The return crossing was quite a bit more difficult, as the wind was up, the waves were showing some whitecaps from an approaching storm cloud, plus we were a little pooped from doing an activity that we weren't conditioned for. The swimmers made it but were laying in the mud trying to get their wind back. The driftwood log was about half way back and barely visible above the waves. Soon it was no longer in sight. That water logged piece of rotten wood had sunk! Panic was about to set in for the log rider. He flailed about briefly but then completely abandoned his log and started swimming – not very well, but he was staying afloat!

Another hand and I started out to get him, but if he hadn't managed to shorten the distance between us, none of us would have made it. We were all totally exhausted. As we got closer to shore the other boys were there to help us. Like many young men, our over estimation of our abilities almost made for some empty bed rolls at the wagon that night. Thank you God!

The gullible young fellow that I mentioned earlier had been flown to the ranch in his father's shiny airplane. All of his equipment was brand new. The new saddle, hat, chaps, and spurs stuck out like a sore thumb compared to the rest of the crew's worn and dilapidated gear. He soon realized that he wasn't fitting in with rest of us, so he commenced trading some of the new stuff for some weathered items.

My old black hat attracted his attention; it had been with me for a couple of years and had survived all the windstorms, wild cow chases, and bucking horses without ever leaving my head. I had a bit of a sentimental attachment to it. First he offered me money for it, but I didn't feel right about taking money for an almost worn out old hat; besides I wasn't going to go bareheaded until the wagon pulled in!

Then he tried to trade me. It did fit, but a straw hat was something I had never worn. There was no way I could keep that thing on in the wind. I'd be getting off my horse and picking it up like he was having to do. An old rancher told me once that he would never hire a man wearing a straw hat because they would be chasing it all the time.

But the young man didn't understand any part of "no" or even "hell no", and continued pestering me about that hat. The cook had a solution for this predicament. He suggested we run a foot race. Winner got the hat. Some of the boys would take the hat over a little hill and bury it in the sand, when they got it buried they would wave to us and the cook would give us the "Ready, Set, Go".

I was told secretly that my hat would be behind the mesquite on the right and something much more foul than my hat would be in the sand pile. About six of the boys took off afoot with the cook's shovel and my hat, while my opponent and I got warmed up for the race in the shade of the wagon fly. We waited,...... and we waited........... It was taking a long time. Maybe the boys were constipated. It is really hard to find crap when you need it.

The kid wasn't much of a distance runner so I had to slow down a little just to make sure he beat me to the pile. He took a high dive into the sand pile and dirt flew everywhere. Laughter was getting the best us; I was drifting over to the mesquite on the right but the high diver saw me and made a quick circle around the bush. I went back to the pile and scratched carefully around the edge. He came in high and fast, this time he went to the bottom and discovered what was really buried there.

Laughter was in total control now, for all of us except one. I was immobilized and some of the boys were completely down. Finally got back to the bush, and no hat! Someone was pointing to a bush on the other side. They hid my hat on their right, not my right. Guess who was approaching the correct mesquite while wiping his hands on his pants leg?

The flying cowboy was grinning as he donned his new, old hat. That was the first as well as last time I lost that hat. Had to wear my wild rag like a bonnet for a couple of days before that two hatted rascal would let me borrow his straw hat.

One of the reasons for writing this story was to make all the readers aware that hanging out with a bunch of mischievous, bored, and rowdy cowhands can be detrimental to your physical and mental well being. Beware of any foot races that involve a pile of sand that must be excavated by hand before claiming your prize. Consider yourself warned!

One cold and rainy Fall gather we had two Texas boys day working at the wagon. They were capable hands, but a little rough on cattle and horses. They fit the mischievous and rowdy part well, but they sure weren't bored. They liked to rope and were pretty good at it, and would lay a trip on one of the horned cows when the boss was not looking. The boss knew about it, but never said anything to them, so they got where they would lay one down even when he could see them. We were a little short handed, but not short enough that we couldn't do without them. It was none of my business, but never understood why the boss let them continue. Perhaps secretly, he like many other punchers, would have liked to flip some old ornery bunch quitter in the air, but commercial interests were a constraint on rough handling of livestock. We were seeing quite a few cows with broken horns; evidence that they had been roped by the horns, the slack thrown over the cow's hip while the roper was turning off to flip the animal around and over. Steer tripping was popular in early days, but due to the damage to livestock it is not practiced very much now.

Socks was a horse that I had started several years prior. He was pretty well broke, but kind of like a playful puppy; his excitement would get the best of him and he would break in two sometimes and take several hard jumps, then throw his head up and trot off. If you weren't paying attention he could sure get out from under you. Socks was in Boyd's string as he was the younger of the Texas lads, and might be more appreciative of a horse like this big sorrel with the stocking legs. Generally, a rider didn't get much information about a horse's disposition or abilities from the boss. They were supposed to take them as they came. However, the crew will share any thing they may know; often the negative information will take precedence over the absolute truth.

He and his partner, Shine, devised a plan for the first ride on Socks. They were going to pony him like the boys on the race tracks do. Shine would lead Socks with Boyd on his back until they felt the pony was warmed up enough to not pitch.

It was a cold, wet morning. The sun was trying to peek through the fog on the eastern horizon when Boyd called for the horse roper to catch Socks for him to ride that morning. I was already saddled and mounted, and as tradition demanded, the first mounted rider would position himself between the rope corral and the boys still saddling up to prevent a frolicsome horse from bucking into the remuda.

The horse roper stuck a neat loop on Socks and pulled it snug around the horse's throat latch. Socks led out willingly, but with a few resounding snorts for sound effects! Boyd bridled him, slipped the rope over his head and dropped it to the ground, turned to lead him between two fellows still waiting for their horses. They stepped on the rope corral and held it to the ground while Boyd and Socks passed over it. After the hobbles were on, next came the cold, wet saddle blanket onto a cold, wet horse's back. A few more snorts and a hump like a Halloween cat, gave a clear indication of things that may come.

Shine took the reins and Boyd removed the hobbles. I thought they would use the hobble rope to slip through the headstall for Shine to lead him, but they didn't. Shine took a dally with the reins, turned both horses around to make sure Socks knew he was no longer hobbled. Boyd climbed aboard and got a good hold of his bucking strap.

They started off, and except for a few little bouncy steps it was going well; for a while it looked like the plan was working. Without any warning Socks announced his intention by breaking wind loudly, took a high jump followed by four more about like the first and stopped dead in his tracks. Shine's horse over shot the landing zone, and the bridle broke away.

I could almost see a grin on Socks when he realized he was free to do whatever he wished.

I expected him to get serious about the bucking, but that wasn't his style. He liked taking a few jumps and then going on with the business at hand. Not knowing what the business was, he decided to run. If they were going to treat him like a race horse he would act like a race horse. He was running pretty hard and every chance he got to jump over a bush he would take it and add a bunch more altitude than he really needed to clear it.

Shine had dropped the broken bridle, took his rope down, and was hot on their heels, Hoped that he wasn't thinking about laying a trip or fore footing them. I didn't join in with the chase, as I knew Socks' mind well, when he had had his fun he would come back to the remuda. Eventually, he did, but first he had to make the most of his little game.

After a hasty repair to the headstall, Boyd and Socks rejoined the drive. That little morning run had warmed up the cold saddle blanket and back well enough. But Socks had to find an occasional booger just to make sure that Boyd still had a good hold on the bucking strap. I don't believe there was any jerk down ropings that day.

Socks would have been up to it, but maybe his pilot – not so much!

Saturday Night on Pitchfork, 1966

Nights on the Town

Most of the stories I have told here have been about the less serious side of ranch life. It was a fun way of life that often overlooks the bad times. The outdoor experiences seemed to reduce the stress levels; there was no rat race. Things were taken in good humor, seeing the wide open world framed between a cow pony's ears was the best perspective I could wish upon myself or anyone else. The bitter cold made the heat of summer more attractive. By the time you tired of the heat it would be autumn again. Each day was a new experience and adventure made better by the changing seasons. You accepted it as a part of nature. “Grin and bear it” would get one through life's uncontrollable events and leave time for what one could control.

During the week from Monday through Wednesday the typical conversation among the single boys was how much fun they had last Saturday night in town, or how drunk they got, maybe even about the pretty girls they danced with. Thursday and Friday their thoughts went to the future. This coming Saturday was going to be even better than the last. A lot more drinking and hell raising. Growing up around these ranch fellows I kind of got the impression that rowdy times in town was a big part of the job description for being a cowboy.

While the wagon works were interfering with about six to eight weekends a year, they felt compelled to make the most of their remaining nights off in town. If there was a rodeo in town every ranch and rodeo cowboy for miles around was in the bars after the performance, doing their part to add to the noise and rambunctiousness. The law would often overlook all but the most grievous offenses The town supported the ranches and the agricultural community supported the town.

One early evening before the rodeo grand entry, an older friend and I were seated on stools at the end of the bar, enjoying a cold one. I knew better, but at the time I thought it was a pretty idea.

Two city cops walked in and loudly asked the bartender if he had any under aged people drinking in here. Lawrence, the bartender said, “No, but you might want to check that fellow at the end of bar.“ as he pointed at me.

“Damn, I'll never shoe another horse for that butt hole!”.

I had shod a couple of horses for free when he did some day work, and he betrayed me like this! Even if I was only seventeen I could shoe a horse, ride a bronc as well as any man in the place. I could go to war and do the work of any man there. I could feel the hackles arising on my back.

The damned government had to pass laws to prohibit things that people naturally wanted to do, and did do when they could get by with it. They were trying to make an outlaw out of me! Or so I thought at the time. I had been breaking horses for almost four years before I could legally buy an alcoholic drink.

The two officers grinned and waved at me, then turned and walked out. I guess that a good bartender not only can pour drinks, but has a good understanding of psychology......Or they were all in on it and pulling my leg?

Tuc City, or Six Shooter Siding as it was once called, had about five bars, two hotels, two restaurants, some boot shops and barbers all within a three block area. I patronized all of them. A nice room in either hotel was about three bucks a night. Getting a shine on your boots cost about fifty cents and you could catch up on the happenings on the area ranches, who got fired and who was hiring. Old Joe could sure pop that shoeshine rag! Drinks, meals, shiny boots, a haircut, a room, and a ton of area news, all for about twelve bucks.

After I got my first car, a '57 Chevy, I didn't have to bum a ride to town anymore, so now I could pass the favor on to another wheel-less puncher.

Jones was a decent hand that had been at the ranch for a couple of months and had wrecked his old pickup,and couldn't afford to get it fixed, so I gave him a ride to town on a week night.

He let on that he was maybe looking for another vehicle. I asked where he wanted to go and he said to just drop him off at the old Central Bar. We agreed to meet there at ten o:clock so we could get back to the ranch before it got too late. I ran my errands and showed back up on time. Jones wasn't there.

It was a slow night at the bar, a couple of railroaders drank up and left, leaving me and the bartender there alone. I suspected that Jones was deep in the middle of a car trade and needed some extra time. The bar man and I were having a good long visit, but every once in while he would go to the door and have a few words with someone then close the door. After the third time he said he had kicked a guy out and told him to stay out, and the guy just kept coming back. Before long the bar tender said, “It's closing time. I don't think your partner is going to show up.”

I told him, “Thanks, maybe I'll check with the police. They might have seen him.”

As I stepped out the door I caught a glimpse of someone leaning against the building down at the corner. Sure enough, it was Jones. He didn't appear to be too drunk but was sure confused. He said he had been trying to git back in that place for over three hours and the bar tender would not let him in.

I asked “Why did you get kicked out in the first place?”

“I'll be damned if I know. Let's go back to the ranch.”

That was all I could get out of him, but I knew there had to be a lot more to this story. Maybe he had sobered up in the three hours he waited outside and couldn't recollect, or just wanted it to be his little secret. Some of these drifting punchers could be weird ducks.

We got to the ranch in time for Jones to take his turn at wrangling horses. I laid on my bedroll without undressing and got thirty minutes of sleep before the breakfast bell went to clanging. Jones had got almost an hours sleep in the car.

Saturday afternoon and night was the social event of the week. You could stand on the corner of Main Street in front of the bank and see almost everybody that lived in two or three surrounding counties. We were well acquainted with local news and events; national and world news was a little harder to come by, but for most of it was not that important anyway at that time.

Frank, the wind mill man who would often visit me at the bronc pens, hauled me to town on a number of occasions. The bronc pens was my world, the pool halls and poker tables were his world. The first stop would be at Manion's Bar on Main. After a few drinks I was ready for a nice steak at the restaurant a couple of doors down the street. Frank was reluctant to ruin a good drunk with eating, and usually wouldn't eat. But I had to get something in my belly besides alcohol. Food really improved my ability to walk and talk on a Saturday night, didn't do much for my dancing though.

Frank would get a game going on the pool table, mostly playing for a quarter. He would win most of them, but miss a shot once in while to keep other player interested. His shots got better as the stakes grew. Once when there was a lot of money on the table the other guy insisted on playing doubles. That's when Frank got me involved. I told him that I couldn't handle a pool cue when I was sober much less now while I'm three sheets in the wind.

He said, "That don't matter, take one shot and I'll do the rest."

So, I did, and so did he. He ran the table. Frank made more money in one night in town than he made all month at the ranch, and he could do it time after time. He stayed with the ranch life because he preferred that to a smokey old pool hall. When he passed he was worth quite a bit of money. I sometimes wonder if he hasn't beaten Gabriel out of his horn in a poker game, and will be blowing it when I see him the next time. That's assuming we both make it. RIP Frank.

There is one more little remembrance of Frank I can share. Once I was doing some prowling by myself in the big Seco pasture on the Bell ranch. That pasture was 70 or 80 square miles big, and I thought I was the only human being in it. The colt I was riding needed some wet saddle blankets pulled off of him and this was a good place to do that.

I jumped a big bobcat out on a flat that had a few small mesquites and not much else. I had always wanted to rope a bobcat, again because of the perceived cowboy job description. So, I shook out a loop and lit in after the kitty. I had ran a few before this but they usually got into the rocks or trees and got away from me.

This cat didn't run very far on the flat ground but bushed up in the biggest little mesquite he could find. I chunked the rope at him, thought it was a miss, but the bush held the loop open and old Tom cat obligingly stepped into it; all the while making angry cat sounds at me.

I had me a cat! Now what in the hell do I do with it? Stories said they would climb the rope and get in the saddle with you and scratch your eyes out. I didn't think my horse was far enough along to ride double with a wild cat.

The tomcat was caught around the middle. We were in a run now to stay ahead in case he decided on a counter attack. The cat was on his side with his head up looking around like he was enjoying the ride. That was a bit troubling, because he was supposed to be bouncing around and being knocked senseless so I could reclaim my rope without numerous lacerations.

Just when I was considering giving my rope to the cat, I saw a blue pickup about a half mile away. It was Frank out checking mills.

He saw me coming at him, and stopped. When he saw what I was dragging he got a shovel and give the the old cat a whack each time I circled his truck, because I wasn't going to slow down as long as that cat was looking around. Finally he was dazed enough for Frank to get my rope off. We moved off a ways and watched. Pretty soon we saw him sneaking off in the brush.

If bobcats communicate with others of their kind, I hope he had as good of a story as I had. Not only was that story told in the bunkhouse, but it even made for some Saturday night conversations.

Shoeing at the Wagon

My First Rodeo

During my high school years I did get in a couple of kid's rodeo's at the local fairgrounds. The only event that appealed to me was the steer riding, I wished they would have had a bronc riding, but steer riding was better than breakaway roping as the only horse I had was a little old and slow for that. Also it was easier to practice for steer riding.

The neighbor boys would come over and we would push a milk cow behind a gate and pull a rope on her. Two of those old cows were a little crazy; they would buck and bawl, sling slobbers every where, and run over anything in the pen. We often had to repair a little fence before dad got home. We knew dad was suspicious, because every time he noticed a loose board on the corral, he would ask me in the kind and tender manner he used when irritated at me, "You damn boys been riding the milk cows again? Don't let me catch you doing that, it'll make them hard to milk." My brother and I had to do the milking anyway, so we reckoned it was worth the risk.

Going back to the steer riding at the fair, I drew the biggest steer in the bunch much to the delight of the other contestants. They were glad they didn't have to get on him – they thought those little ones would be a lot easier on them. That old big steer stepped out of the chute, hesitated a second or two, then took off at a run to the far side of the arena. I got off on the fence, and my reward was sitting on a horse right beside me!

The Rodeo Queen had taken pity on me and offered me a ride back to the chutes behind her, riding double on her horse. She was pretty shiny! What better reward can you give a bashful teenage boy?

It was a jackpot with the winner taking all. I didn't win anything because another boy's steer bucked a couple of jumps before running off, and the rest bucked off. However, I had enough incentive to pursue my rodeo dream.

After graduation from high school I got a ranch job because I really enjoyed eating regularly, ranches fed well, and had lots of horses to ride.

One of the boys in the bunkhouse had an old association bronc saddle without a horn, and a cracked tree. I don't know if the rodeo bronc riders still do that, but the thinking was it would take some of the jar out of the bucking. A little flexibility in the saddle was helpful on a ten second ride (it has since been shortened to eight seconds), and wouldn't hurt a horse's back in that short time, but a broken tree was not good for normal riding. I took many a ride on that old saddle on the bunkhouse floor trying to get my spurring lick perfected.

The Fourth of July was when many ranching towns had a celebration with a rodeo, most were one day events, but Clayton, NM, had a two header. That was two shots at the money, so that's where I went.

In the past year I had been riding a bunch of three year-old colts and some renegade old ranch horses. I was of the opinion that I couldn't be bucked off (I eventually changed my mind about that).

I strapped that old association saddle on a big bay gelding standing quietly in the chute, took my rein measurement and was ready for my first real rodeo!

The pickup man, Bob, was a fellow I had known for sometime. He worked on a neighboring ranch, and was a good hand. One of his most noticeable characteristics was his loud voice. You always knew when he entered a room, or a building, and sometimes even the county! He could be heard just about anywhere he was.

Bob and I had worked together once. I was day working at a ranch where he was a steady hand. One day while making a drive in the river pasture the foreman dropped Bob off in the Canadian River bottom. He whirled his horse around and headed in a hard run for the biggest thicket of salt cedars, and disappeared into them. The foreman waited about a minute, then told me, “Jim, I guess you can follow him”.

The Canadian river was once a wide, shallow river, but a huge dam had been built about twenty miles upstream from where we were. That ended the big floods, and the river developed a narrow channel. The tamaracks had taken over on the wide flood plain. It was easy to miss the bushed up cows during a gather. It took some good brush-poppers to get them out.

Bob had a head start on me, but I took the foreman's words literally, He said to follow Bob . So, I did. He was trying to lose me in the brush. About two miles downriver Bob came out of the river bottom and rode up on a hill overlooking the river. I was right on his tail. We were well ahead of the drive, and, of course, we let some wise old cows double back on us. Later we had it all to do over, but Bob didn't try to outrun me through the brush this time.

Back at the rodeo arena, as I was getting down on my horse, Bob wished me well – from the other side of the arena. When the chute gate cracked open, old Bay took his head and exploded over the partially opened gate. I knew then that I was on a professional bucking horse, and not one of those rinky dink ranch broncs. I felt more power in his every jump than I had ever experienced before. He was a clean bucker, no suck backs or spinning, just hard ground jarring jumps. The bay horse could have jumped out from under me about anytime he wished, but he stayed under me so he could punish me a little more. By this time I was kind of wanting off of him, and wishing this was over.

Then I heard Bob holler, "JUMP, JIM!"

I jumped, thinking he was right beside me. While in the air I caught a glimpse of Bob coming in fast from about thirty feet away. Caught him by the foot just before his horse knocked me over. The realization hit me that I really needed to work on my dismounts. That was something I never had to do on the ranch. We rode them until they stopped.

The next day's horse, and dismount went better. I waited for Bob to get along side of me and in full view before jumping

To my surprise they gave me the biggest check for the bronc riding, which was about a month's wages. After a brief celebration that night I figured out what I'd do with the rest of the prize money. I ordered a hornless association saddle tree from a company in Utah, some skirting and latigo leather, along with a sheep skin, and saddle hardware. I built my first bronc saddle! I wasn't about to put any spur tracks across that new saddle seat either.

A ride with a Rodeo Queen, a first place check, and a new saddle had me totally hooked on bronc riding for the next six years!

Photo by Grace Keith

Dad, Me, and the truck used to haul horses,dogs,and kids.

Photo by Martha Downer Ellis

Moving Camp, Fall Wagon, 1961

Author on the right

Remembrances of November 22, 1963

During the Fall of 1963, I was working on one of the roughest country ranches in eastern New Mexico. Twenty nine miles of rough dirt road and another twenty six miles on a narrow highway to town.

No telephones of any kind. The only contact was an occasional visitation by a neighbor or a small AM radio with limited reception. The day started about 4am and lasted until late afternoon. Trips to town were only attempted when absolutely necessary. What few hours of daylight remaining were usually used in repairing tack or horses. Yes, we repaired horses - doctoring wounds, shoeing, etc.

The ranch had only a few "jeep" trails. So everything was done on horseback. This ranch was not as large as many in the area but, if it were mashed flat it would have been huge …. it was all up and down.

We were gathering remnants that the previous owner had not been able to round up. This required us to put in some long days on horse back. These crafty animals had successfully evaded every roundup for years. The Brahma crossbreeds could navigate that rough country as well as the mule deer and the newly planted Barbary sheep, and were just as hard to capture. Several hundred head of cows with calves, yearlings and bulls were hiding out there in the rocks and pinon trees, and had never been touched by a human hand. Our job was to end their feral life style because any gentler cattle put in the same pastures would soon pick up the their wild habits.

Our cook, Mr. Heman, was a recovering alcoholic when liquor was unavailable, but the recovery stopped when he got to town. Sober, he was obsessed with cleanliness. He scrubbed everything in the cookhouse over and over. I think he hated cowboys but short term cooking jobs were all he had to finance his next binge. He also hated house flies. If he wasn't scrubbing he was stalking flies, swatter fully cocked. He was deadly with it too. If a fly lit on your biscuit, he got it! Consequently we ate with one hand and shooed flies away from our plates with the other. Every meal was coffee, beef, taters and frijoles; breakfast sometimes had a little pork added, the coffee was fresher too. All were pretty good - most meals taste good to a tired and hungry man. But, in the back of our minds, we were always wondering how many flies had been swatted on the mashed taters.

We were short on horses. The kind you could do something on were getting leg weary from the long hard rides. I had three green broke colts in my string but they couldn't take the long hard days and you were almost afoot if you had to drag a three year old slick eared bull out of the brush. So I wrangled horses on them. A little hairy sometimes running the creek bottoms in the dark with defective steering on a pony that wanted to pull a runaway with every little bunch of horses you jumped. But it saved the broke horses for the cattle work.

This particular morning we had gathered about thirty head of mixed cattle, mostly unbranded cows, calves, yearlings, and a couple of bulls in their prime. We aimed them toward a little trail down into a deep canyon which would eventually end up at the main shipping pens.

Contrary to most people's mental image of a cattle drive there was no whooping and hollering; we tried to be as quiet as possible and not rush anything. Most of the crew was in the lead to prevent a runaway down the canyon while only a couple of boys discretely following to foil some wise ol' heifer from doubling back. These were wild animals ...getting them to go was not a problem, stopping them was! If you could keep them from running and herded together you had a good chance of getting them penned. Then it happened! A good hand, but one unfamiliar with this particular trail had failed to anticipate a splinter point and some yearlings made a run for it. The whole bunch began to breakup and the chase was on. Out numbered almost four to one it was impossible to keep track of all the scattered cattle in the brushy canyon. But after a couple of hours we were able to get all of them back together except for one bull which bushed up in a dense thicket of mesquite and cedars. We left him for another day for some cow dogs to get him to abandon the thicket. It was that or a . 30.30 bullet and butcher knife.

We got them penned finally in a big pipe corral with water and hay in it, which they ignored for several days. They stood in the middle of the pen with their butts together, heads and horns outward in a classic wild cattle defensive stance.

Needless to say we were worn out, nothing like pedaling a tired horse to really poop a fellow out. We and the horses had been running on adrenaline for the last several hours. As we made our way to the saddle house to unsaddle, the manager's wife came running down the hill yelling something about the president.

She gave us the terrible news about John Fitzgerald Kennedy getting killed in Dallas. We were shocked and no one said anything, which was unusual because normally everybody would be retelling their version of today's wild cow chase. Like zombies we began the climb up the hill to the cookhouse, each trying to process the bad news in his own way.

Heman, from his vantage point in the cook shack above the horse pens would always keep an eye out for our late arrival and would have dinner on the table by the time we had our faces and hands rinsed off. Today the table was bare! Heman was scurrying around the room with the fly swatter attacking flies on the windows and muttering something about "the damned Cubans". Where he got the idea that Cuba was involved in the assassination I don't know, maybe from the early speculative radio recounts of the tragedy. We suspected he may have had a drink or two because there was an empty vanilla extract bottle on the table.

Finally one of the boys asked "Where's dinner?"

Heman responded not with the expected, "It's in the oven, I'll get it on the table in a minute" but he absolutely erupted,

"THE WHOLE DAMNED WORLD IS GOING TO HELL AND ALL YOU DAMNED SONS A BITCHES CAN THINK OF IS YOUR STOMACHS!!

I must confess ... I would have to plead guilty to that!

Catching Horses

The horse ropers were men that knew every one of the horses by the head, rump, or anything in between which presented it self. The rope corral held about a hundred and twenty head or more. If all the hands went after their own horse with ropes swinging the herd would have learned just how fragile the rope corral was. While in the bronc pen they were taught to respect a single rope stretched just below their chests.

The roper's quick hoolihan loop would settle neatly over the head of the horse that the riders would call out. The two ropers would be the last to get their horses caught. If caught deep as this picture shows most were a little reluctant to lead out, and may need some pretty good tugging.

The remuda was driven into this corral three to four times a day. If there was a trap (small pasture) nearby to keep the horses over night, the last of the days penning was to catch a couple of night horses to wrangle in the morning. They would spend the night hobbled in the corral. Otherwise the night hawk would spend the night on horse back with the loose horses. This method worked well as I never heard of any outfit losing all their horses.

Throwing the Hoolihan

Crossing the Canadian River

Farmer Broke

The Fall cattle works were finished, the calves were weaned and shipped, the chuck wagon was pulled in and stowed in its shed at the ranch headquarters. The extra horses that were to be turned out for the winter had their shoes pulled and hooves trimmed. I rolled my bed, loaded my saddle, and headed for town. The day working was done for this year.

After Thanksgiving festivities with family I unrolled my bed at a bachelor friend's house. In days gone by he had been a good bareback rider, but now his only rodeo event was team roping. He had taken up farming for a living and was running about forty mother cows on the fields of the farm. My plan was to shoe a few horses, maybe start some colts, and help him with the cows when needed; then go back to the rodeos when Spring arrived.

We fit together pretty well, he needed a cook and I needed a roof over my head. Now my cooking leaves a lot to be desired but compared to his, he really thought it was great. Any man soon tires of eating beans out of a can. We now dined on fried taters, hamburger, and gravy. Occasionally, we would find a ring neck pheasant along the fence rows or in the stalk fields and I would pop him the head with my .22 caliber six shooter, and we dined in style! We told everybody that was brave enough to eat with us that it was wild chicken!

We were settling in well for the coming winter. Had some colts to ride and it was looking like I could survive the winter. That and horseshoeing gave me plenty of excuses to get out of the cotton picking. Farming is an admirable profession but it wasn't anywhere in my long range plan. Without farming we would not have any beans, taters or gravy, and we would be forced to be totally carnivorous.

The mail man finally caught up with me and delivered my last months mail – about four letters, all hand written except one, which looked mighty official. It started out with "Greetings from the President........ Lyndon B Johnson". I had a new job with the government in the Department of Army and was to report for duty right after the first of the new year. That gave about two weeks to get all my affairs in order.

The day before I had picked four big stout colts off a ranch about fifty miles to the west. Thought I had plenty of time to get the farm pens set for a bronc schooling operation, but now had to do a little revising of my plan. There was only one corral on the place to keep the horses in and to start them out. My idea was to split the one big pen into two so we could have some one-on-one time with each colt, but there was no time for that now. My potential swamper was busy picking cotton, so this was going to be a one-man operation with no help from a helper mounted on a broke horse.

Surprisingly, those colts acted very well the first couple of days riding in the pen among their partners, despite having a pedigree that was famous for being rank. Not much bucking at all. It was their first trip outside the pen that concerned me. This wasn't like the ranch lands where there was a lot of wide open spaces for a horse to indulge in freedom of expression. There were barbed wire fences, canals, ditches and electric wires everywhere, not to mention all various pieces of farm machinery. A swamper sure would have been nice to have!

The first three that I rode outside went very well. I was thankful that they had been handled when they were weaned and halter broke. So, it was not difficult to avoid all the farm obstacles. However, there is always one that has to be an exception.

Number four was a good looking blue colt with a lot of "go". In fact, he had too much "go" and no whoa! He had a muscular neck along with a bad memory - he didn't remember much of his halter breaking experience. We hit an electric fence wire and took it out; it would have added a little more color to this story if it were fully electrified, but it wasn't and "Old Blue" never even noticed it.

Now we were headed down a rutted road toward a good fence with five strands of barbed wire. Blue would feel this if he hit it head on. Luckily the wire gate was open. After a long run we were now in a pasture well away from the farm fields and had some freedom from unnatural obstacles.

The rolling hills covered with "bull cod" rocks were a good place to convince Blue that he couldn't run forever. He was starting to show some signs of wanting to slow down, but I continued to urge him on. One thing I knew was that it may be difficult to stop a runaway horse but you can make him want to stop by letting him go until he doesn't want to go any more. When they think it's their idea, they'll stop. Some humans are like that as well.

Blue found some reserve energy and we were sailing along pretty well. He had been watching where he was putting his feet during most of this runaway, but one slip up is all it takes to create a memory. He stuck both front feet in a badger hole!

In the split second that followed, I remember flying through air, the first contact with the rocky ground was my forehead, then the lights went out. No, I didn't pass out, but I could feel a lot of pressure on my head and I couldn't see!

Still woozy from the crash I managed to sit up, but was afraid to feel my face with my hands. My racing mind was telling me that my eyeballs were popped out of my head or my forehead scalp was folded down over my nose. These were just some of the possibilities for this terrible situation.

It seemed that I sat there for quite a while trying to figure things out. Nobody knows where I'm at, it may be days before someone finds me - a blind man crawling around aimlessly, not knowing whether it was night or day, sniffing the ground for a bug to eat. If Blue survived he would go home to the ranch where he was raised - might take weeks for people to notice a riderless horse. In this time of draft dodging, this was a helluva way to get out of going to the Army! Some had to go all the way to Canada, I just had to go for a little ride! Those were some of my thoughts as I sat there pondering my future.

Finally after mustering up every ounce of courage I had in me, I tentatively raised my hands to my chin. Felt more like drool than blood, so proceeded further. Mouth was fine. As my apprehension continued to grow, just above the nostrils I felt something strange; Damn! It was the brim of my hat!

There ensued a brief moment of extreme relief followed by a mental butt kicking for being so stupid, but it did feel great to see the light again!

A quick check found the crown of my newest felt hat had a hole in it. The shirt my Mom made for me several years ago had a big rip across the front, the preexisting elbow holes were now too big to satisfy my standards of proper dress. Looking back, I think that I could have been the model for the cover of a modern Western Romance novel, without ripples, of course.

Old Blue was laying on his side breathing a little rough. Wrecks like this frequently end up with broken legs, but his looked fine. I politely asked him to get up with the toe of my boot planted along side his rump, and after a few hesitant steps, he appeared to be fine. Just had the wind knocked out of him. I wondered if maybe he was having some of the same weird thoughts similar to mine.

We headed back to the house. I was leading him at walk until I was satisfied he was sound enough to ride. Tried kicking him into a trot, but he didn't want that. We were about eight miles from the house and I was anxious to get home to repair the new hole in my hat and change my shirt while there was still some daylight. It could get pretty chilly about sundown, and I hadn't worn a jacket on this mild December day. About all my shirt was good for now was a grease rag for the farmer.

After a lot of thumping we got into a long trot but never made it to a lope. His all go and no whoa had gotten reversed. Eventually we came to compromise on that, but not this day.

In those times, I didn't mind a horse pitching with me, but had grown weary of the runaways. As one old cowpuncher told me, "Those Paul Revere rides can be a booger!"

I was proud that I had discovered a quicker way to break a horse of running away, but in all the following chances to use that new found knowledge, I decided not to jerk the front legs out from under a runaway.

Too hard on clothes!

This drawing by the author entitled “**Movin' Camp**” was inspired by a photograph taken by Harvey Caplin. It tells a powerful story of days with the Bell wagon in the 1940's. A time when batwing chaps were more common than shotguns or chinks. Blue denim was fairly new and usually only worn by the younger hands.

They were all "Hands". They knew what a cow was thinking before the cow did! They could get along with about any horse - pitching or stampeding! Their hats may have been dirty and past due for an oil change, but still showed the pride of a man that made his living on a horse.

The Hoodlum was finishing the breakfast dishes while the bedrolls were being loaded. Horses had been wrangled, roped and saddled, the day wrangler had already started the remuda towards the next camp. The rope corral would be stowed in the bin below the chuck box. When the team was hitched the Cosinero and Hoodlum would follow the remuda. The boys would follow the wagon boss to begin another drive to the next roundup grounds.

A fine Spring day !!

Chicken fried steak at the wagon

Bull Hauler

Joe and I had hired out to help gather mavericks off a rocky, and brush covered ranch that had been largely neglected for years. The elderly gentleman who owned it had passed on, and now his estate had leased the place to the people we were helping. There was no telling how many feral cattle remained. They had an airplane flying to get a count on the remnants, but the thick brush hid a lot of them. Roads were mostly unusable and the corrals, except for the main head quarters pens, were in bad shape. It was going to take some good cowboys and some time to clean the remnants out.

Since it was leased the new operators were reluctant to repair anything that cost money except what was absolutely necessary to get the job done. It was wild and beautiful country with plenty of grass, but water was a little scarce. There were a couple of wild cow traps that would have taken quite a bit of ground work to make them functional. The boss decided against repairing them because he would have to build roads to them. So there was nothing left to do but ride out and pick up what we could each day. Some days we might get four or five, other days maybe twenty head and then drive them to headquarters. Cows with calves were put in a pasture down on the flats where it would be easier to gather them for shipping.

One day eleven of us started out, and as luck would have it, we gathered eleven maverick bulls that looked to be about three to five years old. They were of mixed breed, but mostly blacks with a lot of Brahma. We got them penned in some pretty rickety wire pens. The boss wanted to brand them there and then drive them to the house so they could be shipped as soon as the brands peeled. Brand inspectors wouldn't let a fresh branded or unbranded bovine off the place of its birth.

We roped them by the head and heeled them, branded and ear marked them. Those bulls were getting pretty snuffy by the time we finished.

The fifteen year-old son of one of the partners in this operation was helping us. He had a nice little paint pony that stood about thirteen hands high. Most of those bulls were bigger than that! He was a little bit of a brat. He thought he could give orders just like his daddy. If he was signing his name on the paychecks we would have listened to him more. Joe was coaching him on his cussing; he knew most of the words, but not the right tune. He was trying to get the rhythm down and practiced when ever he could.

The boss threw the gate open while we were getting in position to hold them up for a little while before starting them down the trail to the house. They charged through the gate, and went eleven different directions. There was no holding them back.

We weren't outnumbered so it was one rider per bull. The chase was on to get them back together. My bull ran a couple of hundred yards to a brush thicket and gave every indication that was as far as he was going for now.

Over the hill from me there came the longest stream of profanity I'd ever heard. I thought the kid was just practicing, the rhythm was getting pretty good, but there was a sense of urgency about it. I topped the hill to see a bull a little taller than the paint pony, and a lot heavier. He was hooking old Paint in the rump at every stride. Fortunately for the horse, the crossbred bull only had rudimentary horns. The kid was screaming now, the pitch was higher and the rhythm was breaking up. I could have added some new words to my vocabulary that day! That bull taught him more about cussing than all the rest of us put together. I got the bull diverted and "saved his ...., ..., damned ass" like the main gist of his tirade had been about.

It took a while but we got them all back together and drove them to the big pipe pens at the house. The kid was following quietly behind the boss until the big gate slammed shut. Then he made a run for the saddle house to get away from the reminders of the day. A day later his daddy took him home.

A little over a week later the new brands were peeling on the bulls now. The boss was sending Joe and me to deliver the bulls to a feedlot about two hundred miles south of us, but Joe had some sort of family emergency that I think he made up to get out of this trip. The old bobtail cattle truck was about my age and not in near as good of shape as I was. It would have been nice if there were two of us so one could walk for help while the other kept track of the bulls. Top speed on that old truck was almost forty miles per hour if it was down hill, and some of it was.

Things were going well until the truck topped out on the *Llano Estacado,* the great Staked Plains of the southwest USA, some of the flattest country in the world. Early explorers had no landmarks to keep their bearing, so they drove stakes into the ground to find their way back. It has been said that you could ride a horse for days and never get out of the boss's site. In the flat lands, where a road could be easily built in any direction, they made all of them go north to south, or east to west. If you are going southwest you will have some hard turns every so often. Also expect some jogs in the road where the earth's diameter changes. Correction lines they are called.

At those hard turns, the bulls would pile up on the stock racks to the outside of the turn. The stabilizer chains across the top of the rack had broken. On the next turn I could see in my mirror the stock rack was really bulging out. That was the first time I ever went around a corner on two wheels at three miles per hour.

It took some walking and scrounging to find enough good wire to tie those chains back and secure the load. I had to be careful because you could go to jail for cutting another man's fence.

Finally pulled into the feedlot at dark. Everybody was gone except for the night watchman; who reminded me of a bar room bully. He said they had been expecting me much earlier, and to back the damned truck up to the loading chute. He was tired of waiting. I told him that he might want to get some gates set before I let the bulls out.

He said he didn't need to, that it was a long way to the end of the alley and he had plenty of time to get ahead of them. Besides, he said, they were building some new pens back there and there wasn't even a gate on the end.

I reminded him one more time that, if it were me, I'd get that alley blocked. He seemed to be getting a little perturbed at this ranch hand telling him how to do his job.

He snapped at me, " Get that damn gate open! I got them!"

So, I did.

The bulls never touched that loading chute, they flew into the alley and landed running into the dark. The watchman ran for his truck and spun gravel everywhere as he headed for the back side.

Don't know if he made it in time, I just closed my tailgate and headed my old pokey truck north, glad to be done with those critters. I had a long way to go before sun up.

Gathering Bulls

A Good Roping Horse

The Mama Mule

For a good portion of my life on ranches, I worked at the headquarters, lived in the bunkhouse and ate my meals at the cook shack. The cook shack was usually a permanent part of the headquarters where the single men ate along with any visitors. Sometimes the main cook was also the wagon cook, but that would leave the fencing crew, the chore boys, wind millers, mechanics, and other help that was not associated with the cattle work without a handy place to eat, so a temporary cook was hired for one of the positions. The really important visitors were fed and bunked in the elegant main house where the owners or manager lived.

Married men on the cow crew and their families often lived in separate housing away from the main ranch. They were assigned the job of taking care of the area where they lived. These camp men were steady, dependable employees that could get the job done without a lot of direct supervision, and they liked it that way; but they often had to work alone unless they had kids or a wife that could help them.

My status had evolved to the point were I was now eligible for a camp job, so one autumn day I moved my family to the West Camp of the AV ranch. It was about fifteen miles from headquarters and the foreman only came around about twice a month, the first of the month to bring my paycheck and again in the middle of the month to see if I was still there or if I needed anything. You couldn't pick up a phone and call anyone in those days.

West camp was situated at the edge of the sand hills with some tight ground along the Ute Creek and covered about twelve square miles of land. With it being fifty miles from town, we didn't run to the store every day, in fact it was only once or twice a month. No electricity when we first moved in but later the electric company ran a line to the house. It was frequently knocked out by lightening.

It was a pretty good place to be back then, now it would be a great place to be!

My job was to tend to 450 head of two-year-old bred Hereford heifers, to see that they had salt and mineral, the windmills were pumping, and mend fence if needed. The fences were pretty good but occasionally the wind would blow a hole underneath one, or a drifting sand dune would cover one up. When the outfit was shipping and branding I made the two in the morning trip to headquarters to help. This place left the bulls out all year so we had calves to wean and brand each time we gathered. The old gentleman that owned the ranch said he would take a rain or a calf anytime.

Late Winter and early Spring was calving time for the heifers as they hadn't been exposed to the bulls until they were about two years old, which made them calve from late January to March. Using this method, the older a cow got, the more irregular it was as to when they would calve, but if they missed a calf it would be less time between calves. It was the first time heifers that required a lot of attention while calving. Other ranchers preferred to control the bull's access to the cows to get more uniformity in their weanling's sizes and weights.

In the late Fall we usually had to start providing supplemental feed to the heifers. This outfit liked to feed cottonseed meal in wooden troughs on the ground. We would feed the cattle three times a week by riding out horseback and the other three working days we would haul out feed to stack in little caches at the feed grounds. Our method of hauling was a wagon and team.

This ranch was in the process of switching over to pickups for all the camp men. Since I was the newest and lowest on the totem pole I never did get a pickup while I was there, but it really didn't bother me much. My mules didn't get stuck as much in the deep sand as their narrow tired two wheel drive trucks did, but they were sure warmer in the winter. I don't believe I have ever been colder than on a spring seat in a slow moving wagon headed into a cold north wind. Now I know why buffalo robes were so popular in the old days.

I never had worked mules before, and did not consider myself a qualified mule man. My first team was a pair of little mules that would weigh about eight hundred pounds each. They were wise and old enough to vote. Slow and Slower was what I called them. Slower was an expert at just getting the tugs tight enough to look like she was really putting great effort into the pull, but the evener on her side had a little droop in it. Still they knew more than I did about being a teamster, and I learned a lot from them, without that experience I would have never made it through the next team the boss brought to me.

One of the first lessons was when the sneaky little team pulled the loaded wagon into a low spot. If they thought it was one pound overweight, they would balk. I'd lay the leather to their butts until I felt guilty, they would do a little jig but never tighten the trace chains. They wouldn't lead either.

Once someone had told me that you could build a fire under a balking mule, so I tried that. Gathered up an arm load of dry sage brush sticks and lit them on fire. Smoke was drifting up near their heads and they were getting a little antsy. Then the chains rattled and the wagon was moving!

Six foot later it stopped moving, the fire was now right under the front axle of the wagon, – a lot of dry wood under there and a half ton of cotton seed meal above that. Slower turned her head and looked at me with a blank stare on her expressionless face. I dived under the wagon, and began slinging sand everywhere until the fire was out. It is times like this that I know exactly how a Cajun fellow felt when he was helping me shoe a rank mule.

He said, “I wish my mamma would've beaten me more when I was a kid, so I would be better prepared for this!”

Cajoling and punishing weren't working so distraction was the next tool in the bag. But how in the dickens do you distract two sleepy eyed mules with their feet planted in the sand bent upon waiting this thing out? It was beginning to look more and more like I was going to have unload the wagon and pack that feed over the hill on my back.

Twisting an ear is a good distraction, but I didn't think that I could twist both of the mule's ears and drive the wagon at the same time. There was some baling wire in the wagon (we never went anywhere without baling wire. It used to be rawhide, then baling wire and now it's duct tape for repairing just about anything). I cut two pieces of wire and tied each of their long ears together, not tight, but just enough that they couldn't shake it off. Didn't want to hurt those big, long, floppy, beautiful ears because I may have to get a hold of them again sometime. To further secure them I hooked the ends of the wire around the head stall, and I went back to the wagon seat.

They stood there bobbing their heads up and down, then made a few vigorous attempts to shake the wire off. They were well synchronized in their movements, they had been a team for a long time. When their lips went to moving, I lifted my lines and clucked to them. They leaned into the collars and easily pulled the wagon up and over the hill. On the down hill side I pulled them up and removed the wire. We were back on good terms now, but I always made certain I had some baling wire with me after that.

Slow and Slower were getting slower now and it was taking a lighter load now each time we hauled feed out. I did like them because, on a cold day, I could tie a colt to the back of the wagon. If I planned my route right when the last batch was unloaded , I would aim them toward the house, tie the lines up, ride the colt back to the house, and be sitting in front of the fire an hour before they showed up at the front gate. The tire tracks they left in the road were amusing, it looked like two big old snakes had been crawling down the road. They did wander quite a bit but never left the road.

The boss said they had two big mules down at South Camp they weren't using; they had a pickup now. One mule was pretty old and the other was pretty green. When I got back to the house one day, those two mules were in the corral along with a third one. He was a big stout mule that the horse trader said was well broke, and a dang good mule! There was also some harness for the two from South Camp, but I had to rig up something for the new mule. The old molly mule was semi-retired. They sent her along just to keep her with her partner.

Caught the green mule, she was a bit fresh, but I blindfolded her with a gunny sack and got her harnessed. The new "well broke" mule couldn't be approached, so I roped him around the neck, and he took the rope away from me! When I got it back I dallied it around the bottom of a corral post. If I had gone higher with the dally this mule would have pulled the post over in that sandy ground. This "dang good" mule was still fighting the rope. I've heard that you couldn't choke a mule down, but this one went down with a thud. By the time he got his wind back he was blindfolded and had a back foot tied up. He had a couple of little hissy fits about the foot rope but soon gave up fighting and just waited for me to get careless and make a mistake.

They were harnessed now. I had to cannibalize a few sets of harness to get the new mule dressed but I was ready to hook them up to wagon. They both had mellowed a little in the time it took to get all the harnessing done. One at a time I led them still blindfolded out to the wagon and hitched them up. It felt like I was sticking my head into a huge bear trap when I reached behind them to hook the traces on the single trees. They allowed me to live through it

Stealthily I climbed into the wagon. My rope was tied to the two gunny sacks that were the blindfolds. When I got the lines ready and my feet braced, I jerked the blindfolds off.

Upon reflection I see some things I should have done differently.

The wagon should have been pointed south toward the straight road with a slight uphill grade for about three quarters of a mile. After a run up the hill it may have made them a little more controllable by the time we reached the top – especially if there had been a ton of feed in the wagon!

But no! I had it aimed north where there wasn't anything but barbed wire fences and gates. They hit the closed gate at an angle and hung the left front wheel on the huge cedar gate post that was buried about four feet in the sandy soil. That stopped them from forward movement but didn't stop them from running, their bellies were close to the ground and their legs were churning up the sand. Barbed wire was flying about, I imagined the mules and me both getting limbs amputated. The big gate post was leaning and the iron wagon tongue was squirming like a snake. Then the post yielded enough for the wheel to disengage, and off we went down to the big meadow were I was to calve the heifers in a month or so.

Pieces of harness and wagon running gear were flopping around as we made our laps around the vega (meadow) with what was left of the wire gate dragging behind. The adrenaline flow was going down. Greenie and Dang It were beginning to respond to the lines somewhat now.

After the wreck the mules were in surprisingly good shape, just some minor cuts and scrapes. One of the mules had a chunk of hoof wall missing but no blood. It would have been nice to have hitched them up again the next day now that I had the edge off of them. Instead it would take two weeks to repair the fences, gates, wagon, and harness that was torn up. Now I also had to pack a little feed on horse back as well. You can bet that I was a little smarter next time that team got hitched!

The new team didn't balk when the load got heavy. They were still afraid of me enough that they would run through and tear up a hundred yards of fence if I asked them to, or if they dreamed it was what I wanted. We were getting caught up on the restocking of sacked cotton seed at each feed ground.

Some of the boys from headquarters came over and helped me gather the heifers and sort out the "piggies" that looked like they would calve the soonest. We put them in the vega that had plenty of good grass, water, and not many places to hide from me. That was to be my office for the next ten weeks.

The boss hired a day worker to do my feeding, so all I had to do was live with those heifers. The boss said to calve them out in the vega, don't bring them to the house, too much disease there! Also he wanted me to be with them from dawn to dark – if they got into trouble in the dark they would just have to wait til morning. For a while it was kind of fun. The string of horses I inherited there were all good rope horses. The fellow before me loved to rope and the horses showed the training he had put into them.

You could roll up on a struggling heifer, fore foot her, and ease her to the ground. The horse would hold her there, I could pull the calf with my piggin' string, clear the wind pipe, remount, give the heifer a little slack, the rope would fall from her feet, and I could be out of there before she got up. All this could be done in just a few minutes. It was important that you didn't rattle the cow too much or she may not claim her baby, then you would have a pen full of dogies to bottle feed.

As the babies got to where they could travel and everything was going well, I would start drifting them to one of the gates to an outside pasture. That was to lighten the pressure on the vega to produce enough grass to feed the next bunch of "piggies". Vegas in the sand hills are usually sub irrigated as the rain water soaks into the sand very quickly and doesn't run off. Any low spot in sandy areas will be the recipient of any water trickling through the sand, consequently they can be fairly drought resistant, but few four hundred acre vegas can support four hundred and fifty cows for long.

Every few days we would prowl the outside pastures to move any soon-to-be mamas to the obstetric vega. It was an enjoyable job, especially the fore footing part, but anytime I had to follow the same tracks day after day it lost some of the glamour.

While I was occupied in the vega the old big mule from South camp had escaped from the horse pasture, since we weren't using her much, and I knew where she was, it didn't seem to be a problem that needed immediate attention. One day my wife was out riding and wanted to do something meaningful instead of just trotting up and down the road. I suggested she go get that mule and bring her back to the house.

She took off at a lope headed east to capture that old mule. It wasn't too long before she came back. She was blubbering, “T...t....that damned mule tried to k...k...kill me!”

No way, I thought. She's an old gentle thing that wouldn't hurt anybody. I got on the wife's horse and was going to bring this old sow home. Didn't have a rope on the saddle as the plan was to just drive her home. I got her located, she was with a little bunch of cows at a windmill.

A heifer was bawling and trying to get near the old mule, but when she did the old gal would lay her long ears back and make a run at the cow. I soon saw the confused baby calf, it was weak, and the cow had a tight bag. That mule had stolen the calf from it's mama and was about to starve it to death!

I charged the mule thinking I could get her mind off the calf, but the wife's horse having prior experience with this mule turned tail and ran when those big teeth and flashing eyes came charging back at us. With no rope or anything to fend off another charge I headed for the house. I wasn't blubbering but I may have cussed a little.

Saddled my own horse, and returned to the windmill. I had a rope now and my .22 caliber snake pistol loaded with bird shot. My old horse stood his ground as the mule came at me. My intention was to make a hole or two in her long ears, kind of like the piercings that women do, but was afraid I would get an eye so I shot her in the chest. She veered off and I got another load of BB's into her hindquarter.

That did the trick, she turned and ran. To reinforce the message I put a couple more in her butt. When I got her roped she reverted back to the sweet old lady she had been. Back at the corral I looked her over well and could only find one little speck of blood, her tough old hide was almost bullet proof. She spent the next five nights in a pen at the house that was high enough she couldn't jump out. By the fifth night the braying had stopped, and we could get some sleep. If you have ever heard a broken hearted molly mule getting weaned from her calve you will know what we went through.

Horrible sounds!

The happy calf and her worried mama were re-united. The baby's wicked step mom never returned. I saw to that.

Jay, the day worker, and I finished up with a prowl through the pastures and brought in a dozen or more heifers to the calving vega. They looked as if they could domino soon. I had been baby sitting and nurse maiding for two months now and was ready to do some different cow work. Hopefully the calving season would be over in a couple of weeks.

As I took a last look for the day through the heifers already in the meadow, Jay went to gather the milk cows and bring the horses into the home corrals. We usually caught our horses that we were going to ride the next day in the evening, and kept them in the pen overnight to save time in the morning. Same with the milk cows so we didn't have to hunt them in the dark.

I noticed the old molly mule wasn't with the other mules and horses. She was standing next to the fence that separated the vega from the horse pasture, and a heifer with a new born were just a few feet across the fence. Molly had found her a new baby!

The over powering maternal instincts in her old heart were creating the desire for an adoption or, rather an abduction once again. Jay came right by her when he brought horses in at a run. Normally she would have fell in with them and come to the house, but she chose to stay with the calf. Jay pulled up and circled back to bring her into the herd. The ears went back and teeth came out in full attack mode. Jay quickly turned back to the other horses while molly continued to chase him for a short way.

Jay had told a few stories about some wild things he had done in his life. Basically they consisted of the three “R's” of cowboying; roping, riding, and wrecks. Apparently, he never had a seventeen hand mule with fire in her eyes make a run at him.

He asked me what he should do about that mean mule. I told him, “Never mind, I'll lope out there and bring her in.” He was wanting to see me get run off too, but I charged out there, slapping my chaps with my hand. The popping noise awakened a memory within her. She broke and ran for the house.

Jay just stood there shaking his head back and forth in disbelief at what he had just seen. I could tell I had moved up on his list of wild punchers. He was so proud of me, the next time he went to town, he bought me a brand new pair of chrome plated Chihuahua style spurs. Which I still have to this day to remind me of him and the Mama Mule.

Never did I tell him of how much gunfire it took to accomplish that little feat. A fellow has to take care of his reputation!

Line Backed Heifer Getting Assistance Through the Gate

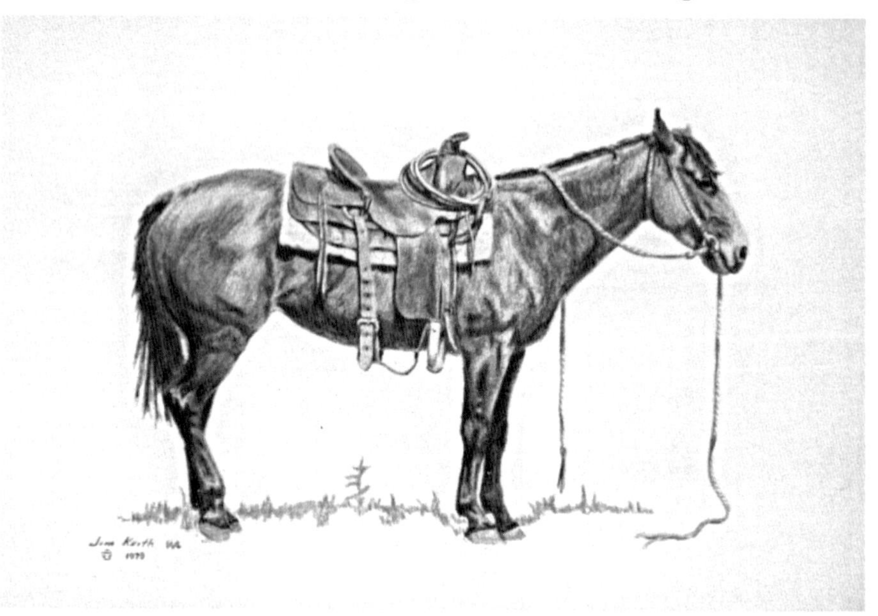

Ground Tied

Bucking Horses and Broncs

Once I was young with good reflexes to handle about any thing a horse could do to me. I remember these times as some of the greatest of my life. That door has closed now, but others have opened with the potential to be even greater. Those early days have left me with many fond memories of some of the best horses but mostly some of the worst as they were the challenges that made memories. It is difficult to recall all the ones I started as there were hundreds of them. At one time the Bell ranch remuda, which usually numbered about 120 horses, had over eighty head that I had started in the bronc pen.

After leaving the Bell I continued breaking horses for other ranches and the general public. My sons helped me during their school years, but when they left home to pursue their own lives, the fun was lessening and I tapered off on colt starting except for some of my own.

Although bucking horses and broncs are synonymous in most people's minds, my use of the word "bronc" usually, (but not always) denotes a green horse or one that had just been started under saddle, while a "bucking horse" was one that continued to buck long after it's training had started. This applied to rodeo horses as well as old spoiled or outlaw horses on the ranches. I enjoyed the broncs until they had the rough edges knocked off, but my favorites were the bucking horses. I can honestly say that I have never suffered a major injury from the broncs, bucking horses and the thousands of horses I've shod over the years.....Well, except for maybe one I'll get to later.

Wednesday and Saturday there was a horse auction in Clovis, NM, and a local stock contractor would buy up a bunch of prospective bucking horses. Wednesday night and Sunday afternoon was when a couple of others and I would go test them. There was a lot of unknown quantities about these ponies, some would run away, some would sull up and not do anything, while others would take a little run on you, then explode. Once in a while one would pitch well enough to make the draw at the next rodeo.

The boys with the bareback riggings would take the smaller horses, and I would strap my assassination saddle on the bigger ones. One day they had more little ones than we had bareback riders, so I tied a knot in my cinch, saddled up and nodded for the gate. The little sucker took a good jump out, then stuck his head under his belly up to about his navel, and went to spinning. He didn't have much withers nor belly for the flank cinch to hold my saddle in place. Every turn he made that saddle and I were moving a little further up on his neck. Finally he shucked us both. Since I was still in the saddle when it hit the ground I didn't count that as a buck off! It was just an equipment malfunction.

A fellow that ran a small preconditioning feed lot brought a big old bay horse in for us to try one Sunday afternoon. I had shod this horse for him several times; the label “puke” fit him pretty well. I was happy to get on him to deal him some misery to make up for all the crap he had given me while shoeing.

He took a run to the middle of the arena so that everybody could see me getting bucked off, and then blew up hard. His belly turned to the sun and I felt my saddle swells getting away from me. He slung me as far as my leg and the stirrup leathers would let me go, then pulled me back under him; my foot was hung up! I got in my version of an alligator death roll, then he pooped me out right between his hind legs.

I retrieved my boot, shook the dirt out of it and limped back to the chutes. Cherokee Lil, the cowboy's favorite bar tender, who had a reputation as quite a bronc rider herself in her earlier days, was perched on the fence next to the chutes.

She softened the blow a little when she said, “Don't worry. Casey Tibbs couldn't have tied his pants on that one and done any better.”

Another Sunday afternoon the contractor wanted me to strap my rig on a good little bareback horse that was losing his enthusiasm for bucking. He thought if I would stick him a little with the spurs then fall off it might help. Falling off wasn't in my job description, so we agreed that the pickup man would move in after about the third jump.

Old Hitler was a little hard to get down on in the chute. He would rear and try to flip over. Finally got my seat and nodded, my spurs were in his shoulders and the pickup man was right there.

The pickup man was mounted on a big stout buckskin horse with a Pitchfork brand on him. He was newly purchased as a heading horse, but today they were trying him out as a pickup horse. I knew a little bit about the thinking of the managers of the big cow outfits.

They didn't sell big geldings in their prime that weren't lame unless they had a hole in them somewhere. We found the hole in old Dunny that day.

Anyway, three jumps came and then fifteen or twenty and no pickup man. I got off on the fence at the end of the arena. Horns were honking and spectators were hollering. Now, I may have made a ride or two in my life that deserved that kind of fanfare, but I didn't think this was one of them.

All that noise wasn't for me, it was for the Pitchfork horse that had sucked back when I stuck my hack rein out for the pickup man. He was still laying spread eagle on the ground with several people fanning him. The next weekend up in the Texas panhandle I won a go-round on Pitchfork. Later he was ranked as the number two horse at a bucking horse auction; he may have been number one had he not bucked his rider off so quick.

Hitler went on to put a few more bareback riders out of the money.

The only time I got laid up for awhile was when a ranch horse that had a reputation for bucking off good riders let me down hard. I had been doing pretty well at the amateur rodeos, and hadn't been bucked off in public so I was sure enough getting a little cocky. This horse had been used as a stud, but was producing too many foals with crooked legs, so he was gelded and eventually ended up in my string.

He could be talked out of pitching, but today, was time to see if he was as good as I had been told. I was leading a few hands down to the south end of the ranch to check on something (memory is a little sketchy here). The horse was feeling a little fresh, I didn't do anything to talk him out of it; I just gigged him with a spur. Suddenly I was on his neck, and he kept me there for about three jumps then flipped me in the air. The first thing to hit the rocky ground was the back of my head followed by my legs on each side of my head. I had been folded at the level of my shirt pockets,-humans are not meant to be folded there. Sixty years later every now and then I feel a stabbing pain between my shoulder blades, and I know old Wilbur, the ex-stud hoss is checking on me.

A month or so later I got a reride on him. Frank, the wind miller, had built us a two horse trailer that would hold about four horses. None of us knew much about trailer dynamics, so when we found out it wouldn't work very well like that, he added another gate to keep the horses up at the front. Yaqui and I were trailered up and going to find a poor cow at the lower end of the Seco.

Yaqui dropped me and Wilbur off, and he was going to drive around to a windmill and start his prowl from there. We were to meet up at the mill later. If we found the cow we would rope it and load it in the trailer. If the cow and horses didn't all fit in the trailer, I would lead his horse home. Little did I know at the time that horse trailers would soon change the nature of ranching. Far less wet saddle blankets now.

Wilbur and I spotted a little bunch of cows over on some sandy ground, so we headed that way. I wondered if old Wilbur could pitch as hard in the loose ground as he could in the rocks. The pony obliged me. About the time we got it all settled we heard a horn honking back at the place we were unloaded. Yaqui was waving and motioning for us to come back. Damn! I knew I would be rolling my bed.

He said we needed to get his horse back to the ranch and sew him up, the horse was bleeding pretty bad. Apparently his horse had turned around in the trailer and the sharp hinges on the middle gate had sliced his knees. Yaqui never said a word about our little rodeo, but I was certain when we got back he would fire me, because there was no way he could have missed it.

After we got the horse stitched up he finally said, "Wilbur a little fresh today?". Almost the same words except for the horse's name he had said a year or so ago when I rode my first Bell horse. I agreed with him, and that was all there was to it.

The Clayton rodeo was always good to me. I could make the pay window on a regular basis there, but as I've heard a number of times, "All good things must come to an end".

My saddle was set and I was ready to come out on a gray mare called Dakota Lil. She wasn't very big, but quick as a cat. I had seen her buck a few times in the bareback riding, she was impressive. If you whistled up on her you had a check. The fellow before me got in a storm and was hurt, and then his horse was running with the hack rein dragging, he stepped on it and took a tumble. We had an injured man, and an injured horse in the arena.

It was taking a while for the ground crew to clear the arena. The announcer was running out of bad jokes to tell, so he started talking about me. He had done a little cooking for a ranch where I was helping clean out remnants. He knew just enough about me to invent some really good stories. He told some whoppers then started bragging on me. I had gone three seasons without being bucked off in a rodeo. Didn't qualify all of them, but I was hard to get on the ground. Many of the others could out show me on a horse, and win the go round money but I won my share of averages.

While the announcer was building me up I realized it was going to be a hard act to follow myself. Forgot to reset my saddle and old Dakota Lil blew out of that chute as hard as any I had been on. I got her marked out, but that was all I accomplished. She grazed the flank man with her first kick out of the box then followed with duck to the left then dove to the right. I was pretty loose in the saddle by then and lost a stirrup. I kissed the arena dirt about ten feet away from the chute.

The announcer agreed to act like he had never heard of me if we were ever in that situation again. We both felt pretty silly.

Cherokee Lil was highly amused when I told her about a horse named Lil that dumped my butt soundly and broke my lucky streak.

I didn't rodeo much in Colorado but did place good enough in one of the CCRA rodeos to earn a spot at their end of the year finals in Lamar. On the way up there I stopped to pick up a couple of friends to ride with me. Clyde was an old time bronc rider that had won the Cimarron rodeo when he was fifty eight years old. Leo had been a rough stock rider for quite awhile. I had some good advisers with me.

We stopped in Raton, NM, for a little drink and ended up spending the night in the bar. Clyde ordered a Salty Dog and since that was the name of the horse that earned me a shot at the finals I felt obligated to try one as well. They were sure good and I kept after them until last call. The viperous drink snuck up and bit me. I have no recollection of anything for the next eight hours.

We arrived in Lamar with a few hours to spare. All the motel rooms were sold out, so we went over into Kansas to get a room, and decided we had time for a nap. Maybe some of the fog would clear out of my head before it was time to saddle up.

It was after eleven o:clock when Clyde shook me awake.

"I think they probably turned your horse out by now."

"Well hell, there ain't nothing left to do but go back to sleep." I did promise myself that I wasn't going to let that happen again. The many well wishers would be hard to face, but nobody was more disappointed than I was.

The XIT Reunion rodeo was one of the biggest and usually best run amateur rodeos in the country. I would try to make it, as often as possible, but it never did fit me well. Something would go wrong. A bad draw or miss marking the horse out were some of the things that were haunting me there. This time I got fouled by my horse at the gate, and got a reride on another horse.

They had built a new arena that sure was nice, and big. It was almost as big as two of most other arenas.. This was Texas, their wide open spaces invites bigness.

Popcorn was my reride, he looked like he might be a decent bucking horse, but looks can be deceiving. He hit a few pretty good licks then took off for the the far end of that huge arena. He could run faster than I would have guessed. This had turned into one of those Paul Revere rides where the front brim folded up against the crown of your hat. There was only one pickup man, and he was getting out run badly. He cut across the arena and as Popcorn and I came flying by I made my jump. I got my hand on the back of his shirt, but I was still going faster than he was. I rolled along on the ground and came up with a good piece of his shirt still in my hand. I apologized for wrecking his clothes and offered it back to him, but he declined.

"Naw, you keep it. It ain't much use to me now!"

If I ever run across him again I will buy him a new shirt.

They offered me another reride, but they were out of fresh horses, so it would have to be one that had already been out, and didn't do very well the first time. I declined. What was the point? All they had was one pickup man, and he was half naked.

A rodeo stock contractor had booked two different rodeos on the same weekend. He split the bucking string, and had Jack, a bull rider, and me take the horses to put on one of the shows. This place furnished their own roping cattle, and they had wild ranch cow riding, so we didn't have to mess with any bovines

The great looking Rodeo Queen (as most of them are) graciously volunteered to help us. It was a unanimous decision, we quickly took her up on the offer. She would be helping Jack and I would go ask her to help me, then Jack would be back to get her. Poor gal got her legs run off trying to work for both of us at the same time.

Jack didn't want to ride a cow, so he didn't enter, but I got in the bronc riding. The two of them were standing together on the platform behind the bucking chute when I nodded for the gate. I didn't score high enough to make it to the money. Jack said I would have done a helluva lot better if I hadn't been looking back over my shoulder keeping an eye on them, and just minded my own business.. Oh well! You can't win'em all!

The Spring of 1963 was when I was getting serious about a career in rodeo. My plan was to fill my permit and get my regular membership card in the Rodeo Cowboys Association. I pointed my old Chevy pickup east to Henrietta, Oklahoma, and enrolled in one of Jim Shoulder's earliest rodeo schools. Once again I was immersed in a world of my heroes

Tommy Tyree and I shared a room there. Tommy was two or three years younger than I, and showed a lot of potential as a bronc rider. He looked good on a bucking horse. Tommy and I were the most advanced students ,so we got some of the best horses. None of the beginner dinks for us, we were riding some of the finals horses.

There were plenty of horses to try. I was on twenty nine head that week and Tommy was right up there. I got bucked off three times, but got two of them ridden the second time around. I really got my money's worth that week.

My biggest problem was I was always a little stiff. Bill Fedderson used to tell me that I had been on too many ranch broncs and was afraid of walking home. It's not a long walk out of an arena. Loosen up! He was right. High school basketball coaches have told me the same thing, “Get that cob out of your butt, and MOVE.” I think that cob is permanently attached and it's still there. However, Tommy didn't have that problem, he just needed to add a few more seconds to his ride.

Tommy rode back with me to Amarillo, but we had to get through Oklahoma City first. My last horse of the week was about as sore as I was and flipped over backwards, whacked me on the ground hard and mashed me some. I asked Tommy to drive, but he was in about the same shape as I was. As we neared OKC, my body was stiffening up pretty bad.

This was before Interstate Highways and side mirrors on pickups.

We hit the city at the height of rush hour on one of the widest, and busiest roads I had ever seen. Cars were zipping past us on both sides, some were honking, and other drivers were giving us the international hand signal of disgust. We finally pulled over on the side to wait out the rush. Tommy and I decided that Oklahoma drivers were ranker than any of Jim Shoulders' bucking horses.

Tommy was a good one. He took things as they come, and handled anything on his plate without a bit of complaining. He filled his permit and got his professional card and was well on his way to making rookie of the year. At least that was what the two month old copy of the Rodeo Sports News was reporting when I got to read it in Germany on the Army base.

Then came the terrible news that Tommy was involved in a scrape, not of his making, and had gotten killed in Las Vegas, Nevada. Rest in peace, Tommy, and thanks for the all too brief times we got to spend together.

Life lived brings good times, fond memories, and sorrow. Tommy could handle it, so must I.

Epilogue

The preceding stories related some of the events of my life from childhood until shortly before my thirtieth birthday. Although the life style was very enjoyable, and definitely something I would have liked to pursue as my life's work, I was concerned about the future of devoting my life to ranch work or rodeo.

Many of my older friends that were approaching retirement age were not much better off than I was financially, and were relying on Social Security as their only retirement income. I felt there were limited opportunities for advancement in the industry. My main interest was with horses and not the cattle side of the business. To me a cow was only there to provide a reason to ride a horse, to teach the horse how to work a rope, and to have something to chase off of rocky bluffs.

After getting blown off of a tank in the Army (non-combat) and injuring my hip, I tried to return to the ranch life. As the next three years passed it became increasingly difficult to tolerate the hip pain that the long hours in the saddle brought about. The injury has only minor effects on other aspects of my life, but it did end my ability to ride a horse for long hours. It didn't affect my rodeo bronc riding, I can tolerate almost anything for eight seconds! What it did change was the extra weight I picked up in the service. I went in at 145 pounds and came out at 175. My center of gravity had moved.

Now I had a family and had to provide a home, something that been of little concern to me in previous years. Life lived produces change, and change has always benefited me in the the long haul. Many changes have occurred in my life over the years, mostly in my vocations and avocations. The main constant is my relationship with horses. Shoeing horses has been with me all through my working life with the exception of military service. Even if I couldn't ride them, I could shoe them without much difficulty. I fluctuated between full time and part time several times through the years. The times I was part time was when I taught classes in farriery and later when I manufactured horseshoes and black smithing tools. But it was still centered around horses. Shod my first horse when I was fifteen and my last when I was seventy-six.

If you have read this far, I sincerely hope that you have enjoyed these stories as much as I have enjoyed reliving them and passing them on to you. Who knows? I may write more about some of the. other doors that have opened for me.

If you liked these stories please leave an honest review on Amazon. If you didn't please let me know:

windyben@snakebite.com

I am looking forward to visiting with you!

New titles to be released soon

Practical horseshoeing. Through the eyes of Jim Keith, CJF.

After sixty years of field experience Jim will give you a new perspective on many of the common problems a farrier may see. Don't expect to see a lot of acronyms, charts or graphs. Just a clear explanation of the bio-mechanics of locomotion, and how trimming or shoeing affect the performance and well being of the horse. With many years of observation and study behind him, Jim's main goal of increasing the useful life span of a working horse has been paramount in his practice.

The author's experience in the field of farriery and his teaching history gives him a valuable insight into the absolute "need to know" categories of the trade. The focus is primarily in that area while providing less emphasis on the "nice to know" areas.

Expect clear explanations of what is happening when we trim a hoof and nail up a shoe.

The Greatest Art works of Contemporary Blacksmiths

Steel and other metals are a powerful medium for the hands of today's artist/blacksmiths. The resurgence of an ancient art form promises a valuable resource for inspiration and documentation of the art.

The editors are currently soliciting "GREAT" color photos of forged metal art for consideration to appear in the book. Please make sure that you currently own the rights to each photo submitted and will allow inclusion in the book if the editors deem it appropriate.

For submissions or questions please send email to"
windyben@snakebite.com

Thanks and Happy Hammering!

Glossary

Bench. A land form on the sloping side of a mountain or mesa that appears as a step or flattened area.

Bosal. A stiff loop of rawhide that goes on the nose of a horse that is attached to the reins to control the animal.

Bull cod rocks. Stones that have been eroded into rounded shapes and are roughly the size of a bull's testicles.

Cantle. The back end of a western saddle at about the hip pockets of a rider.

Cosinero, Spanish word for "cook".

Cheek. A rider that pulls by the head stall, the head of a horse towards him to prevent the horse from moving while mounting.

Dogies. Orphaned calves or foals.

Drive(s). Term used for for a round up or relocating of livestock.

Frijoles. Spanish for "Pinto beans".

Hackamore. A head stall, nose band (bosal) and reins,.usually used on young horses before they are acquainted with a metal bit.

Headstall. Normally a leather strap used to hold the bit or bosal on the horse's head. A bridle.

Hoodlum. Cook's helper.

Hoolihan. A method of throwing a lariat that does not require much spinning of the loop before releasing it.

Huerfano. Spanish for "orphan".

Kack. An old saddle.

Nurse cow. A good milker that will allow dogies to nurse.

Prowl. Riding out to check on cattle conditions.

Remuda. A herd of broke horses on a ranch.

Snuffy. An aggressive action from livestock. Blowing snot.

Stomper (bronc). Horse breaker or rider of the rough string.

Swamper. Rider on a broke horse to assist the bronc rider.

Untrack. A few steps taken by a horse to realize that the restraints have been removed.

Walking on egg shells. Tentative steps taken by a horse that indicates all is not well in his mind and it is not comfortable

Wild rag. Scarf or bandanna usually worn around the neck

The Team

Waiting On the Herd

Vigil Canyon

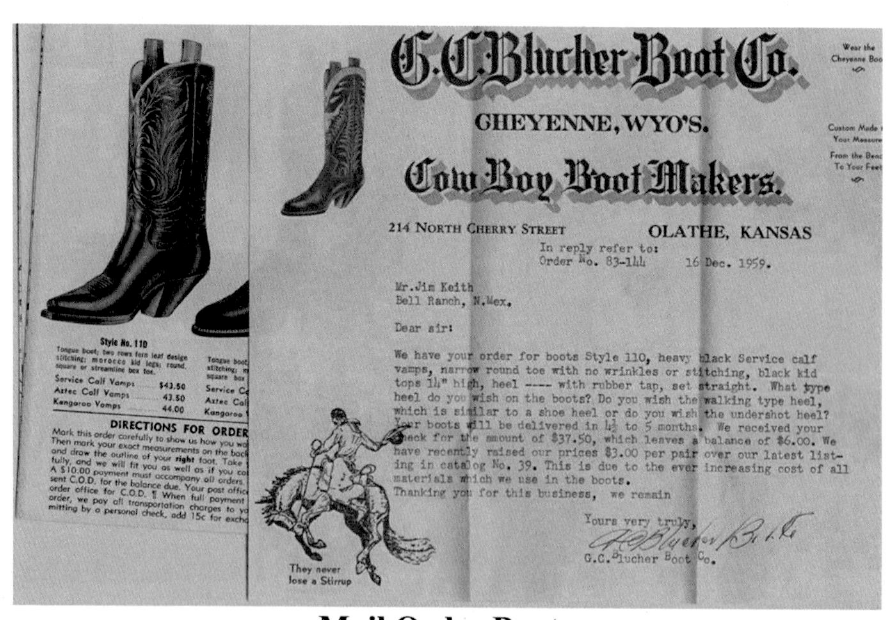

Style No. 110
Tongue boot; two rows fern leaf design stitching; morocco kid legs; round, square or streamline box toe.

Service Calf Vamps	$43.50
Aztec Calf Vamps	43.50
Kangaroo Vamps	44.00

DIRECTIONS FOR ORDER
Mark this order carefully to show us how you wa
Then mark your exact measurements on the back
and draw the outline of your **right** foot. Take
fully, and we will fit you as well as if you co
A $10.00 payment must accompany all orders.
sent C.O.D. for the balance due. Your post offic
order office for C.O.D. ¶ When full payment
order, we pay all transportation charges to yo
mitting by a personal check, add 15c for excha

G.C.Blucher Boot Co.

CHEYENNE, WYO'S.

Cow Boy Boot Makers.

Wear the Cheyenne Boo

Custom Made Your Measure

From the Benc To Your Feet

214 NORTH CHERRY STREET OLATHE, KANSAS

In reply refer to:
Order No. 83-144 16 Dec. 1959.

Mr.Jim Keith
Bell Ranch, N.Mex.

Dear sir:

We have your order for boots Style 110, heavy black Service calf vamps, narrow round toe with no wrinkles or stitching, black kid tops 14" high, heel ---- with rubber tap, set straight. What type heel do you wish on the boots? Do you wish the walking type heel, which is similar to a shoe heel or do you wish the undershot heel? Your boots will be delivered in 4½ to 5 months. We received your check for the amount of $37.50, which leaves a balance of $6.00. We have recently raised our prices $3.00 per pair over our latest listing in catalog No. 39. This is due to the ever increasing cost of all materials which we use in the boots.
Thanking you for this business, we remain

Yours very truly,
G.C.Blucher Boot Co.

They never lose a Stirrup

Mail Order Boots

Damp Day on the Spade

Water Hole

Longhorn Cow

Puncher

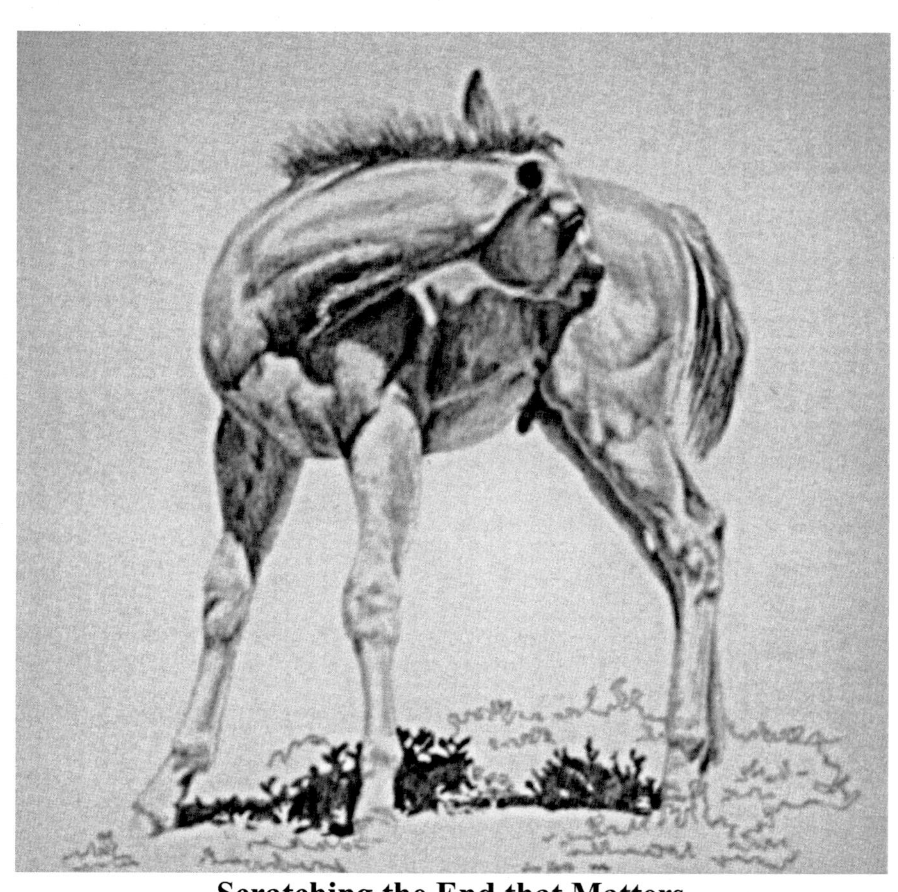

Scratching the End that Matters

Made in the USA
Columbia, SC
12 July 2023

20336941R00062